teacher's friend
publications

D0127368

December!

a creative idea book
for the
elementary teacher

written and illustrated
by
Karen Sevaly

Copyright © Teacher's Friend,
a Scholastic Company
All rights reserved.
Printed in the U.S.A.

ISBN-13 978-0-439-50380-8
ISBN-10 0-439-50380-9

This book is dedicated
to teachers and children
everywhere.

Table of Contents

Making the most of it!

WHAT IS IN THIS BOOK:

You will find the following in each monthly idea book from Teacher's Friend Publications:

1. A calendar listing every day of the month with a classroom idea and mention of special holidays and events.

2. At least four student awards to be sent home to parents.

3. Three or more bookmarks that can be used in your school library or given to students by you as "Super Student Awards."

4. Numerous bulletin board ideas and patterns pertaining to the particular month and seasonal activity.

5. Easy-to-make craft ideas related to the monthly holidays and special days.

6. Dozens of activities emphasizing not only the obvious holidays, but also the often forgotten celebrations such as: Santa Lucia Day and Kwanzaa.

7. Creative writing pages, crossword puzzles, word finds, booklet covers, games, paper bag puppets, literature lists and much more!

8. Scores of classroom management techniques and methods proven to motivate your students to improve behavior and classroom work.

HOW TO USE THIS BOOK:

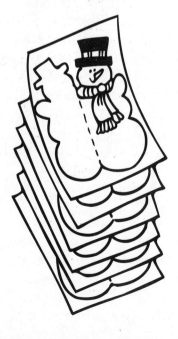

Every page of this book may be duplicated for individual classroom use.

Some pages are meant to be copied or used as duplicating masters. Other pages may be transferred onto construction paper or used as they are.

If you have access to a print shop, you will find that many pages work well when printed on index paper. This type of paper takes crayons and felt markers well and is sturdy enough to last. (Bookmarks work particularly well on index paper.)

Lastly, some pages are meant to be enlarged with an overhead or opaque projector. When we say enlarge, we mean it! Think BIG! Three, four or even five feet is great! Try using colored butcher paper or poster board so you don't spend all your time coloring.

MONTHLY ORGANIZERS:

Staying organized month after month, year after year can be a real challenge. Try this simple idea:

After using the loose pages from this book, file them in their own file folder labeled with the month's name. This will also provide a place to save pages from other reproducible books along with craft ideas, recipes and articles you find in magazines and periodicals. (*Essential Pocket Folders* by Teacher's Friend provide a perfect way to store your monthly ideas and reproducibles. Each *Monthly Essential Pocket Folder* comes with a sixteen-page booklet of essential patterns and organizational ideas. There are even special folders for *Back to School*, *The Substitute Teacher* and *Parent-Teacher Conferences*.)

You might also like to dedicate a file box for every month of the school year. A covered box will provide room to store large patterns, sample art projects, certificates and awards, monthly stickers, monthly idea books and much more.

BULLETIN BOARD IDEAS:

Creating clever bulletin boards for your classroom need not take fantastic amounts of time and money. With a little preparation and know-how, you can have different boards each month with very little effort. Try some of these ideas:

1. Background paper should be put up only once a year. Choose colors that can go with many themes and holidays. The black butcher paper background you used as a spooky display in October will have a special dramatic effect in April with student-made, paper-cut butterflies.

2. Butcher paper is not the only thing that can be used to cover the back of your board. You might also try fabric from a colorful bed sheet or gingham material. Just fold it up at the end of the year to reuse again. Wallpaper is another great background cover. Discontinued rolls can be purchased for a small amount at discount hardware stores. Most can be wiped clean and will not fade like construction paper. (Do not glue wallpaper directly to the board; just staple or pin in place.)

3. Store your bulletin board pieces in large, flat envelopes made from two large sheets of tagboard or cardboard. Simply staple three sides together and slip the pieces inside. (Small pieces can be stored in zip-lock, plastic bags.) Label your large envelopes with the name of the bulletin board and the month and year you displayed it. Take a picture of each bulletin board display. Staple the picture to your storage envelope. Next year when you want to create the same display, you will know right where everything goes. Kids can even follow your directions when you give them a picture to look at.

ADDING THE COLOR:

Putting the color to finished items can be a real bother to teachers in a rush. Try these ideas:

1. On small areas, watercolor markers work great. If your area is rather large, switch to crayons or even colored chalk or pastels.

   (Don't worry, lamination or a spray fixative will keep color on the work and off of you. No laminator or fixative? That's okay, a little hair spray will do the trick.)

2. The quickest method of coloring large items is to start with colored paper. (Poster board, butcher paper or large construction paper work well.) Add a few dashes of a contrasting colored marker or crayon and you will have it made.

3. Try cutting character eyes, teeth, etc. from white typing paper and gluing them in place. These features will really stand out and make your bulletin boards come alive.

   For special effects, add real buttons or lace. Metallic paper looks great on stars and belt buckles, too.

LAMINATION:

If you have access to a roll laminator, then you already know how fortunate you are. They are priceless when it comes to saving time and money. Try these ideas:

1. You can laminate more than just classroom posters and construction paper. Try various kinds of fabric, wallpaper and gift wrapping. You'll be surprised at the great combinations you come up with.

   Laminated classified ads can be used to cut headings for current events bulletin boards. Colorful gingham fabric makes terrific cut letters or bulletin board trim. You might even try burlap! Bright foil gift wrapping paper will add a festive feeling to any bulletin board.

   (You can even make professional looking bookmarks with laminated fabric or burlap. They are great holiday gift ideas for Mom or Dad!)

2. Felt markers and laminated paper or fabric can work as a team. Just make sure the markers you use are permanent and not water-based. Oops, make a mistake! That's okay. Put a little ditto fluid on a tissue, rub across the mark and presto, it's gone! Also, dry transfer markers work great on lamination and can easily be wiped off.

LAMINATION:
(continued)

3. Laminating cut-out characters can be tricky. If you have enlarged an illustration onto poster board, simply laminate first and then cut it out with scissors or an art knife. (Just make sure the laminator is hot enough to create a good seal.)

One problem may arise when you paste an illustration onto poster board and laminate the finished product. If your paste-up is not 100% complete, your illustration and posterboard may separate after laminating. To avoid this problem, paste your illustration onto poster board that measures slightly larger than the illustration. This way, the lamination will help hold down your paste-up.

4. When pasting up your illustration, always try to use either rubber cement, artist's spray adhesive or a glue stick. White glue, tape or paste does not laminate well because it can often be seen under your artwork.

5. Have you ever laminated student-made place mats, crayon shaving, tissue paper collages, or dried flowers? You'll be amazed at the variety of creative things that can be laminated and used in the classroom or as take-home gifts.

PHOTOCOPIES AND DITTO MASTERS:

Many of the pages in this book can be copied for use in the classroom. Try some of these ideas for best results:

1. If the print from the back side of your original comes through the front when making a photocopy or ditto master, slip a sheet of black construction paper behind the sheet. This will mask the unwanted shadows and create a much better copy.

2. Several potential masters in this book contain instructions for the teacher. Simply cover the type with correction fluid or a small slip of paper before duplicating.

3. When using a new ditto master, turn down the pressure on the duplicating machine. As the copies become light, increase the pressure. This will get longer wear out of both the master and the machine.

4. Trying to squeeze one more run out of that worn ditto master can be frustrating. Try lightly spraying the inked side of the master with hair spray. For some reason, this helps the master put out those few extra copies.

LETTERING AND HEADINGS:

Not every school has a letter machine that produces perfect 4" letters. The rest of us will just have to use the old stencil-and-scissor method. But wait, there is an easier way!

1. Don't cut individual letters as they are difficult to pin up straight, anyway. Instead, hand print bulletin board titles and headings onto strips of colored paper. When it is time for the board to come down, simply roll it up to use again next year. If you buy your own pre-cut lettering, save yourself some time and hassle by pasting the desired statements onto long strips of colored paper. Laminate if possible. These can be rolled up and stored the same way!

   Use your imagination! Try cloud shapes and cartoon bubbles. They will all look great.

2. Hand lettering is not that difficult, even if your printing is not up to penmanship standards. Print block letters with a felt marker. Draw big dots at the end of each letter. This will hide any mistakes and add a charming touch to the overall effect.

   If you are still afraid to free hand it, try this nifty idea: Cut a strip of poster board about 28" X 6". Down the center of the strip, cut a window with an art knife measuring 20" X 2". There you have it: a perfect stencil for any lettering job. All you need to do is write capital letters with a felt marker within the window slot. Don't worry about uniformity. Just fill up the entire window height with your letters. Move your poster-board strip along as you go. The letters will always remain straight and even because the poster board window is straight.

3. If you must cut individual letters, use construction paper squares measuring 4 1/2" X 6". (Laminate first if you can.) Cut the capital letters as shown. No need to measure; irregular letters will look creative and not messy.

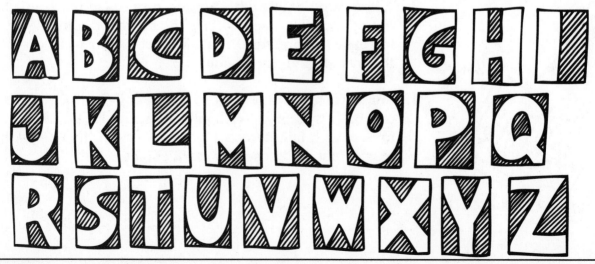

Calendar

December!

TF1200 December Idea Book

DECEMBER

1ST ROSA PARKS, a black seamstress, began the American Civil Rights Movement by refusing to give up her seat on a Montgomery, Alabama bus. (Discuss with your class how this and other events in the 1960s changed life in the United States.)

2ND On this date in 1823, the MONROE DOCTRINE was declared by President James Monroe at his annual address to Congress. (Ask students to find out what this policy meant to the United States and Latin America.)

3RD English astronomer WILLIAM HERSCHEL discovered the planet Uranus on this day in 1781. (Ask students to locate Uranus on a map of the solar system.)

4TH Mexico celebrates the DAY OF THE ARTISANS in honor of the country's laborers. (Ask students if they know which day Americans honor their laborers.)

5TH WALT DISNEY, creator of Mickey Mouse, was born on this day in 1901. (Show the class one of Disney's nature films in celebration of the day.)

6TH Today is SINTERKLAAS DAY in the Netherlands. (Ask students to say Sinterklaas fast, ten times. The children will soon see how he came to be called "Santa Claus" in the United States.)

7TH Today is the anniversary of the bombing of PEARL HARBOR by the Japanese in 1941. (Ask students to ask parents or grandparents where they were on that day.)

8TH ELI WHITNEY, American inventor, was born on this day in 1765. (Ask students to find out what he invented and what it meant to the history of the United States.)

9TH The famous American clown EMMETT KELL, was born on this day in 1898. (As an art project, students may wish to paint their own clown faces in celebration.)

10TH Today is UNITED NATIONS HUMAN RIGHTS DAY! (Ask students to list what they consider to be basic human rights.)

11TH UNICEF was established on this day in 1946. (Instruct students to find out what this organization does and what the letters U.N.I.C.E.F. represent.)

12TH INDEPENDENCE DAY in Kenya was declared on this day in 1963. (Ask students to research which country ruled Kenya before it declared its freedom.)

13TH Today in Sweden, people celebrate SANTA LUCIA'S DAY with a special candlelight parade. (Students may wish to make Santa Lucia headwreaths in celebration.)

14TH The SOUTH POLE was discovered on this day in 1911 by the Norwegian explorer Roald Amundsen. (Ask students to research the event and trace his voyage on the classroom map.)

15TH The BILL OF RIGHTS became a part of the United States Constitution on this day in 1791. (Read it aloud to your class. For a copy on full-sized parchment paper, contact the General Services Administration, Washington D.C., 20408.)

16TH On this day in 1773, American colonists dumped British tea in the Boston Harbor. This event was known as the BOSTON TEA PARTY. (Ask students to find out what the colonists were protesting.)

17TH ORVILLE and WILBUR WRIGHT made the first successful airplane flight in 1903. The flight lasted only 12 seconds. (Students might like to see if paper airplanes can stay aloft as long.)

18TH On this day in 1865, the 13th AMENDMENT to the U.S. Constitution was ratified. (Select a student to read it to the class and discuss its meaning.)

19TH In 1958, President Eisenhower greeted the world on the first RADIO VOICE BROAD-CAST from space via satellite. (Explain the concept of satellite transmission to your class.)

20TH In 1803, the United States purchased more than a million square miles of territory from France for $20 an acre. (Ask students to locate the territory known as the LOUISIANA PURCHASE on the classroom map.)

21ST Today is FOREFATHER'S DAY in honor of the pilgrims who landed at Plymouth, Massachusetts in 1620. (Ask students to find out how many days they spent on their journey.)

22ND Today is WINTER SOLSTICE, the shortest day of the year. (Ask students to locate the time of sunrise and sunset in the local newspaper.)

23RD   On this day in 1975, President Ford signed the METRIC CONVERSION ACT. (Ask students to measure their height using both standard and metric measurement.)

24TH   The Christmas song "SILENT NIGHT" was composed and first sung on this day in 1818. (Find the story of this special night and read it to your class.)

25TH   Today is CHRISTMAS DAY! (Assign a country to each student and ask them to find out how their country celebrates this special day.)

26TH   Today is BOXING DAY in Great Britain, Canada, and some countries in Europe. (Ask students to find out how it is celebrated and why they call it "Boxing Day.")

27TH   The famous French chemist LOUIS PASTEUR was born on this day in 1822. (Ask students to research his discoveries.)

28TH   CHEWING GUM was first patented by William Semple on this day in 1869. (You may like to permit gum chewing in class for this one day in celebration.)

29TH   Today marks the anniversary of the WOUNDED KNEE MASSACRE. More than 200 native Americans were killed by U.S. soldiers on this day in 1890. (Ask students for their thoughts on the struggles of the American Indians.)

30TH   Congress authorized the minting of a new HALF DOLLAR on this day in 1963. (Ask students whose portrait is displayed on this coin and why?)

31ST   Today is NEW YEAR'S EVE! (Ask students to list resolutions the world could make in order to better the life of all humankind.)

DON'T FORGET THESE OTHER IMPORTANT HOLIDAYS:

HANUKKAH   (Celebrated on the twenty-fifth day of the Hebrew month of Kislev.)

KWANZAA   (The last week of December beginning on the 26th.)

 TF1200 December Idea Book

December Calendar Symbols

December

Sunday	Monday	Tuesday	Wednesday	Thursday	Friday	Saturday

December Activities!

Holiday Word Find

ACTIVITY 1

UNSCRAMBLE SANTA'S REINDEER NAMES.

ZNETILB   _ _ _ _ _ _ _

PDIUC   _ _ _ _ _

XINVE   _ _ _ _ _

HSREAD   _ _ _ _ _ _

MOTEC   _ _ _ _ _

CANDRE   _ _ _ _ _ _

DULOHPR   _ _ _ _ _ _ _

CRNEARP   _ _ _ _ _ _ _

DDNORE   _ _ _ _ _ _

If you need help.... Dasher, Dancer, Prancer, Vixen, Comet, Cupid, Donder, Blitzen and Rudolph!

ACTIVITY 2

CAN YOU FIND ALL OF THE DECORATIONS FOR THE TREE?

CANDYCANES, ORNAMENTS, ANGEL, TINSEL, STAR, BOWS, BELLS, GARLAND, ICICLES, LIGHTS and PINECONES

```
L K I J H O P L L L M N B V C S T A R H N J K O P
W C V G H J B O W S S D F G Y T R E D F V B N M K
S D R T G F H R Y N J H U I K D E R T I G T Y H J
G G T Y H J U N R E W Q R T Y U I K L C D R T Y U
A D E R T H C A N D Y C A N E S K L J I D F T F G
R F T Y J G H M N B Y N A L R U D R T C F G Y U M
L F G T H Y N E J K R E W X Z A N G E L M J G Y R
A D E R T Y H N D F B C F R T Y H J H E G H N M K
N F T F T G H T I N S E L B H J U I L S D R T S X
D F G T H Y U S K I L O J E F T G H U J N B V C X
P I N E C O N E S T Y H N L G Y U I P R E W D S F
B G H U Y T F G H J U I K L G V B N M K L P O I U
S E R T H J U I O K J M N S E D C V B N M K J U Y
S E R T G F V B H J K L I G H T S E W R T F G H J
A S D C V B N M K J H G F D S A T R E W Y U I O P
R F D E S W Q A Z X C V B N G Y T U I J K L O P U
```

My Letter to Santa!

_____
date

Dear Santa,

_____

_____

_____

_____

_____

_____

_____

_____

_____

_____

_____

_____

_____

_____

Signed _____

MY
SANTA BOOK

Name_____

TF1200 December Idea Book

Holiday Trivia

To play Holiday Trivia, first enlarge this Christmas Tree Gameboard onto posterboard or draw the tree on the class chalkboard. Next, divide the class into two teams, the RED team and the GREEN team.

To start the game, toss a coin to see which team will go first.

Each team has separate questions and answers. When a team lands on a numbered space, refer to the corresponding numbered question. If the team answers the question correctly, they may move to the next space. If the answer is incorrect, they must give up their turn.

The object of the game is to see which team can get to the top of the tree first.

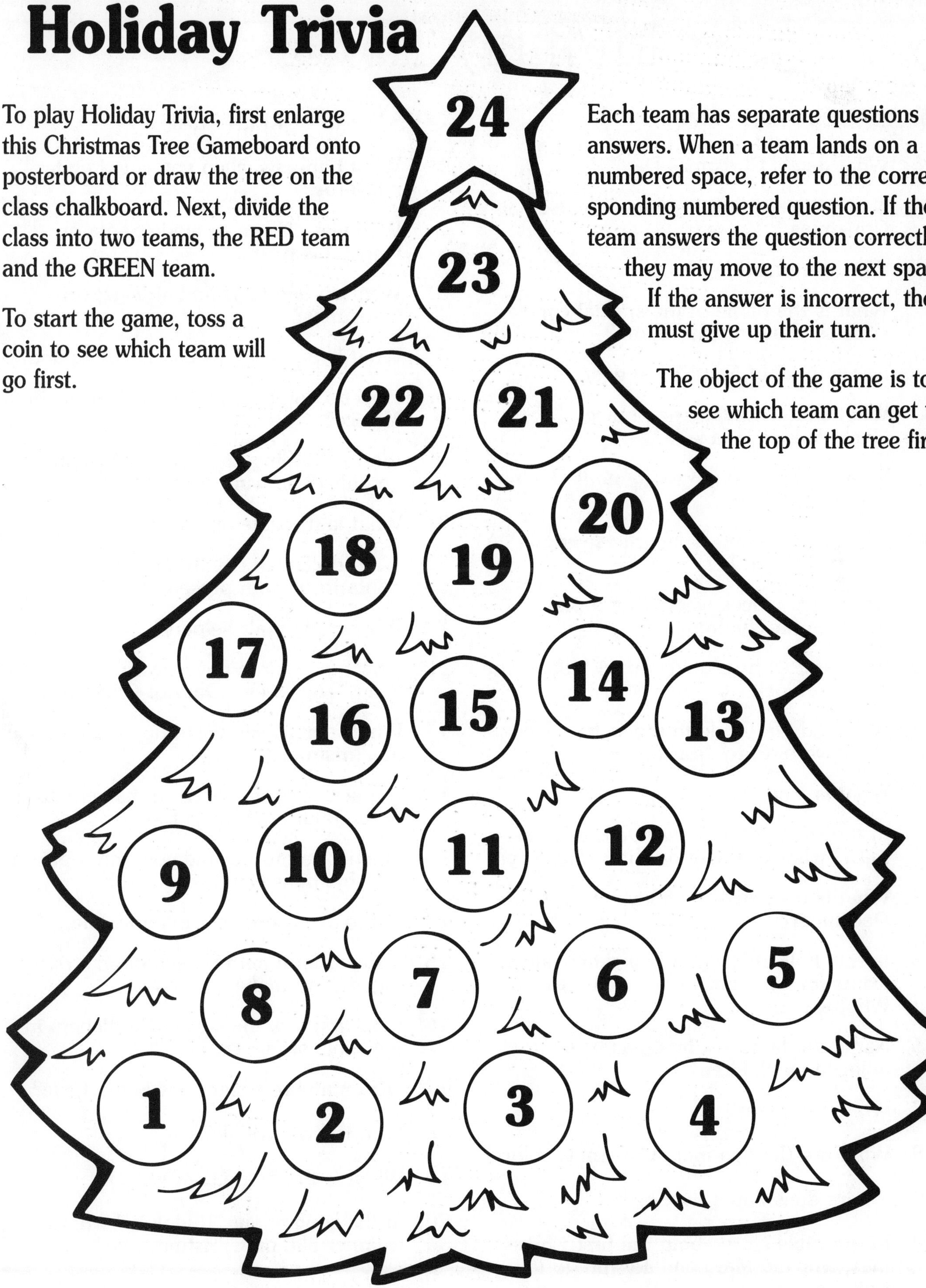

24

23

22   21

18   19   20

17   16   15   14   13

9   10   11   12

8   7   6   5

1   2   3   4

Holiday Trivia

QUESTIONS - RED TEAM

1. What day is Christmas Day?

2. Name the red flower commonly used at Christmas.

3. Who were the Magi?

4. What is the name of the special candlestick used during Hanukkah?

5. Name three of Santa's reindeer.

6. What song contains the phrase "Fa-la-la-la-la-la-la-la-la?"

7. What is the name of the famous singing chipmunk?

8. What was Scrooge's favorite saying in "A Christmas Carol?"

9. Name two places where Santa puts presents for children.

10. In what country would you wish someone "Joyeux Noel?"

11. What did Mary ride to the stable where she gave birth to Jesus?

12. What is a creche?

13. In the song "The Twelve Days of Christmas," what was sent on the eighth day?

14. What is the Jewish holiday celebrated in December?

15. In one holiday song, a boy claims all he wants for Christmas are two things. What are they?

16. Name the famous Christmas ballet enjoyed by children.

17. What are latkes?

18. What are the two main Christmas colors?

19. Where does Santa live?

20. In the Bible story about the first Christmas, why did Mary and Joseph go to Bethlehem?

QUESTIONS - GREEN TEAM

1. What happens when you stand under mistletoe?

2. Who was chosen to guide Santa on Christmas Eve?

3. What do bad boys and girls get for Christmas?

4. What is Santa Claus called in England?

5. How do you say "Merry Christmas" in Mexico?

6. Who's "nipping at your nose" when you go outside in winter?

7. What is the date of Christmas Eve?

8. What do Dutch children leave out for Santa to fill with presents?"

9. Who are Santa's helpers?

10. How many turtle doves were sent in the song "The Twelve Days of Christmas?"

11. What famous snowman do we sing about at Christmas?

12. Name one of the three spirits who visited Scrooge on Christmas Eve.

13. In what country would you find a piñata on Christmas Day?

14. Name one ingredient in mince pie.

15. Name a food item people often string together to make garlands.

16. Who first saw the star of Bethlehem in the Bible story?

17. How many reindeer does Santa have?

18. Who is Kris Kringle?

19. When is the first day of winter?

20. In the song about "Rudolph," what is the weather like on Christmas Eve?

Holiday Trivia

QUESTIONS - RED TEAM (continued)

21. What do people hang on their doors at Christmas?

22. What is said that animals do on Christmas Eve?

23. What is "roasting on an open fire" in "The Christmas Song?"

24. Name three words Santa says when he's happy.

QUESTIONS - GREEN TEAM (continued)

21. Who is "coming to town" in the popular Christmas carol?

22. What is the "top" called that Jewish children play with?

23. What is the name of the little disabled boy in "A Christmas Carol?"

24. Name one of the gifts brought to Jesus by the Three Wise Men.

ANSWERS - RED TEAM

1. December 25
2. Poinsettia
3. The Three Wise Men
4. Menorah
5. Dasher, Dancer, Prancer, Vixen, Comet Cupid, Donder, Blitzen and Rudolph
6. "Deck the Halls"
7. Alvin
8. "Bah, Humbug!"
9. Under the tree and inside stockings
10. France
11. Donkey
12. Replica of the stable where Jesus was born
13. Eight maids a-milking
14. Hanukkah
15. Two front teeth
16. "The Nutcracker"
17. Potato pancakes which are made during Hanukkah
18. Red and Green
19. The North Pole
20. They went to be counted and to pay taxes
21. Wreaths
22. They talk
23. Chestnuts
24. "Ho, ho, ho!"

ANSWERS - GREEN TEAM

1. You get kissed
2. Rudolph
3. Coal in their stockings
4. Father Christmas
5. Feliz Navidad
6. Jack Frost
7. December 24
8. Wooden Shoes
9. Elves
10. Two turtle doves
11. Frosty
12. The Ghosts of Christmas Past, Present and Future
13. Mexico
14. Raisins, apples, cinnamon, cloves, nutmeg, sugar, and sometimes meats.
15. Popcorn and cranberries
16. The Three Wise Men
17. With Rudolph, nine
18. Santa Claus
19. December 22
20. Foggy
21. Santa Claus
22. Dreydl
23. Tiny Tim
24. Gold, Frankincense and Myrrh

Snowman Math

7 x 4 =

6 x 3 =

3 x 3 =

SNOWMAN MATH

Start the holiday season with this clever math idea.

Cut several snowmen from white paper. Label each one with a different math problem. Tape the snowmen to popsicle sticks and write the answers on the bottom of the sticks.

Decorate a shallow box with holiday wrapping paper. Cut slits in the box with an art knife and insert each stick so that the answer is hidden.

Students can solve the math problems and then pull the snowmen to check their answers.

You can also create several matching activities for young children by making several copies of the snowmen and coloring them different colors. Ask the children to match the snowmen that have blue hats or red mittens, etc.

Snowman Story

_____

_____

_____

_____

_____

_____

_____

_____

_____

_____

_____

_____

Santa
Color
Page

TEACHERS: Add your own math problems to Santa. Children can color the picture when their work is completed.

Elf Wheel

Cut out and assemble this "Elf Wheel" with a brass fastener. Cut out the two rectangles, as shown.

Add your own math problems and answers to the wheel on the next page. Move the candy cane to reveal the answer.

cut out

cut out

Make one for each child in class. They will love learning their multiplication tables with "Mr. Elf."

12   2x6

TF1200 December Idea Book

Dreaming of the Holidays...

_____

_____

_____

_____

_____

_____

_____

_____

_____

_____

_____

_____

_____

_____

_____

_____

_____

Santa's List

Create a great holiday bulletin board by enlarging this cute Santa. Children can write their own names on Santa's list as a welcome to classroom visitors.

Amount I have
to spend:

$ _____

MY SHOPPING LIST!

Name	Gift	Amount
_____	_____	_____
_____	_____	_____
_____	_____	_____
_____	_____	_____
_____	_____	_____
_____	_____	_____
_____	_____	_____
_____	_____	_____
_____	_____	_____
_____	_____	_____
_____	_____	_____

Total $ _____

For Goodness Sake!

Award Ornaments

Decorate the classroom Christmas tree with these "Award Ornaments."

Copy the ornaments onto colored paper. Students receive an award for each assignment they complete.

for a great job!

Congratulations!

Name

Good Work!

Name

After coloring the ornament, children can hang it on the tree.

(Paper clips that have been stretched out make good ornament hangers.)

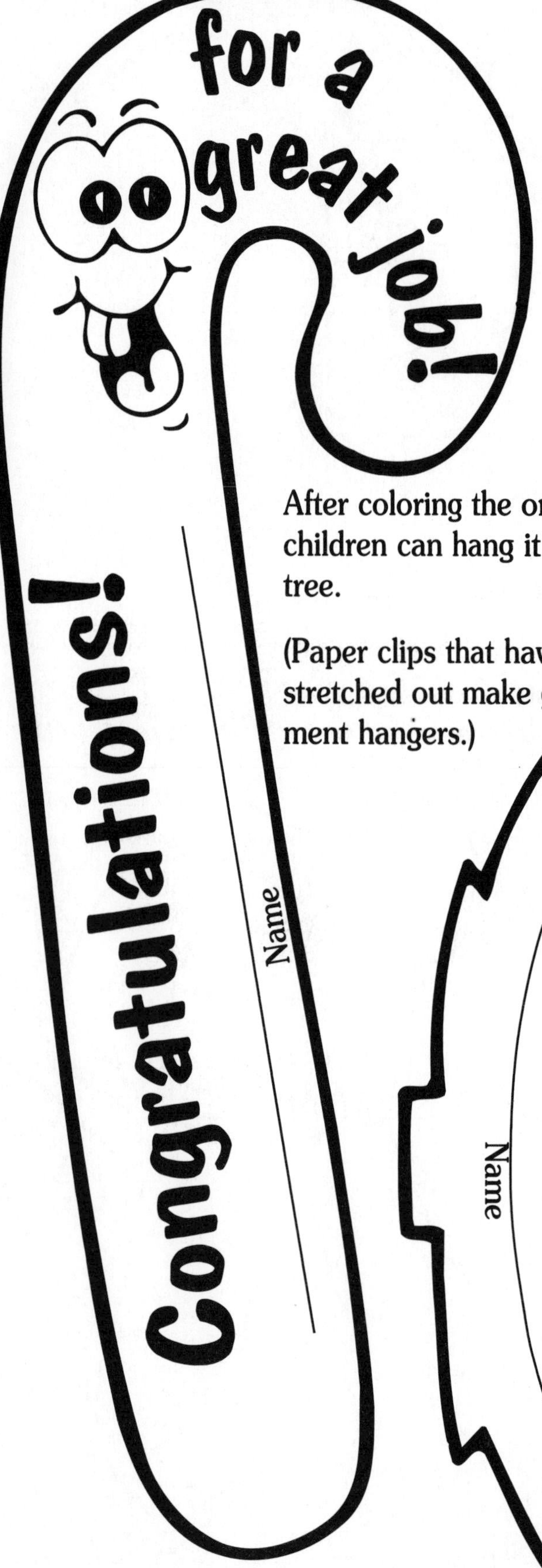

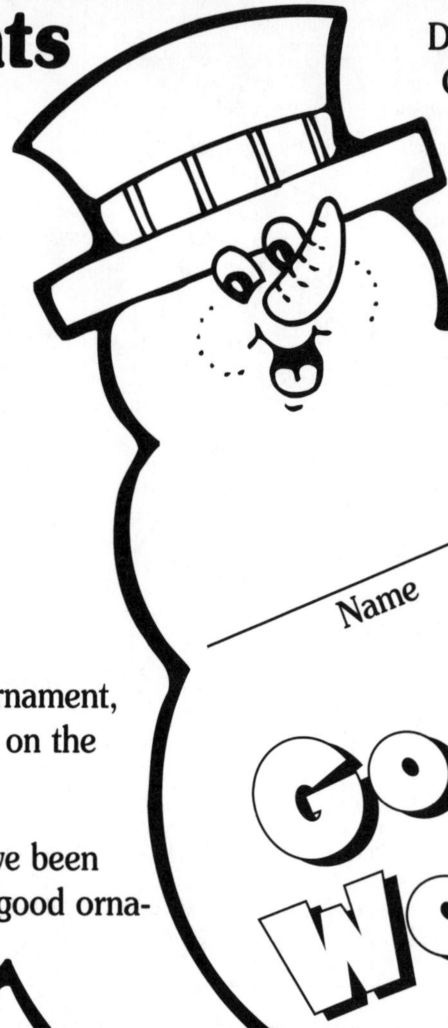

SUPER STUDENT!

Name

Name

Really Did Great in School Today!

Date

Name

Was a Perfect Santa's Helper Today!

Date

Name

Was A Wonderful Student Today!

Date

Teacher

Name

Was A Real Joy in Class Today!

Date

Pencil Toppers

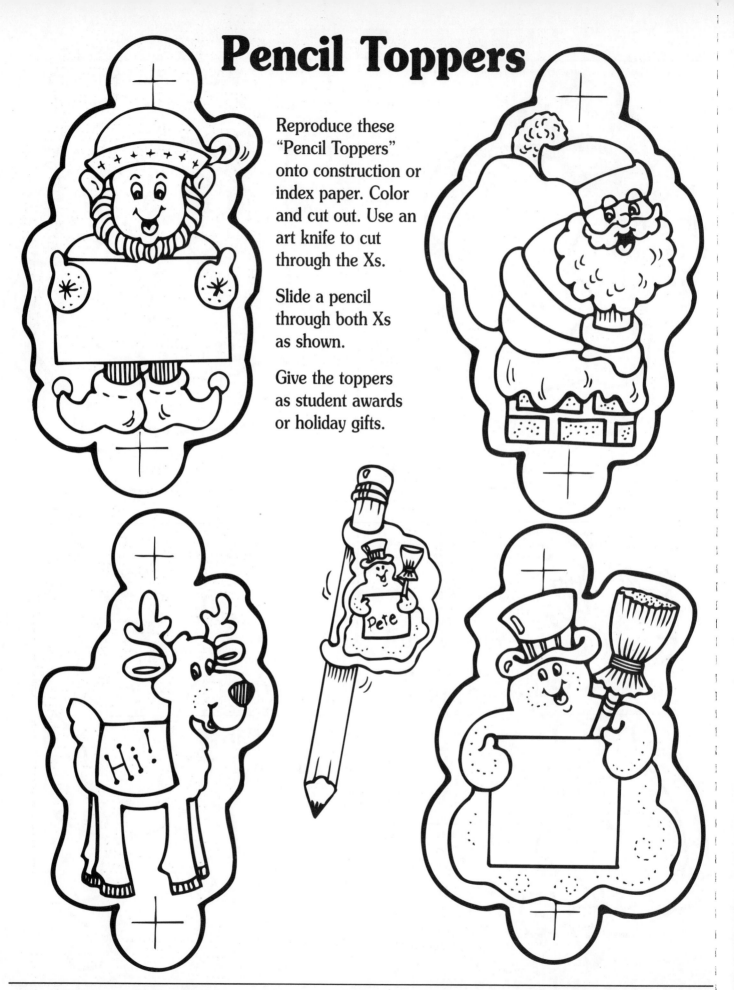

Reproduce these "Pencil Toppers" onto construction or index paper. Color and cut out. Use an art knife to cut through the Xs.

Slide a pencil through both Xs as shown.

Give the toppers as student awards or holiday gifts.

Pete

Hi!

Holiday Mini Booklets

FOLD   FOLD

FOLD

FOLD

SKI INTO THE LIBRARY FOR GREAT READING!

Name

Happy Holidays!

Books... a special gift!

Corner Bookmarks

Santa

Copy these corner book-
mark patterns onto heavy
paper and color with
crayons or markers.
Laminate them if you wish.
Cut the patterns out along
the heavy black lines and
fold along the dotted lines.
Tape the back flaps together
where they meet.

Name

Bell

Place the corner book-
mark over the corner of a
page in any book. (A
great gift idea!)

Name

Super Student Award

presented to

_____
Name

for

_____

_____

_____

_____   _____
Teacher   Date

Good Citizenship Award

presented to

_____
Name

for

_____

_____

_____   _____
Teacher   Date

DECEMBER
STUDENT
OF THE
MONTH

NAME

SCHOOL

TEACHER

DATE

Holiday Carolers

Enlarged, these cute carolers can be used in bulletin board displays. You might wish to write holiday greetings on each song book cover. Or, wish visitors to your class a Merry Christmas in several different languages.

In this size they can be used as gift tags or even bookmarks.

You might even like to enlarge one of them to posterboard size and attach it to the classroom door. A "Happy Holidays" and room number would be all you would need.

However you choose to use them, you'll find that they bring a very festive spirit into any classroom.

Holiday Finger Puppets

Use these cute finger puppets as awards for good behavior or completed work.

Simply color and cut out each puppet. Bend the puppet around your finger and tape into place.

Students will be eager to do creative writing assignments with these finger puppets as motivators.

Ask each child to choose a puppet and write a story about it. Students can act out their stories in front of the class.

Stocking Awards

Name

Make copies of this stocking pattern and have each student decorate their own.

Pin the stockings on a bulletin board depicting a fireplace and mantel.

Toy Patterns

Make copies of these toy patterns and award them to students for good behavior or improved work habits.

Students can place the toys in their personal stocking using the pattern on the previous page.

Holiday Crafts!

Angel Ornament

Color and cut out this angel pattern. Bend the angel face forward and bring the ends of her dress together in back. Staple the ends together. For a special touch, add cotton or angel hair to the wings and glitter to her dress. Attach a string to the top of her halo to hang from the tree.

Santa Ornament

Cut out and fold this Santa on the dotted lines. Tape the sides together to form a pyramid shape. Hang by a thread as a tree decoration or stand on a table as a mini center piece.

Glue cotton on his beard for a fuzzy effect.

More Holiday Crafts!

RUDOLPH DOOR DECORATION

Instead of traditional door wreaths, have your students make these charming paper bag reindeer.

Using a large folded grocery bag, tape the bottom corners as shown. Children can use crayons or paper scraps to add the eyes. A bright red pom-pom can be glued in place for his nose. Cut ears and antlers from brown construction paper and tape to the back of the bag. Have children add their own holiday greeting.

A smaller version can be made using a small lunch sack instead of a large grocery bag.

SNOW SCENES

This holiday craft will be a cherished possession for years to come.

For each Snow Scene you will need the following:

   Baby food jar
   Spray paint
   Florist clay
   Plastic holiday figure/greenery
   Silver glitter
   White glue

Paint the lid of your baby food jar and let dry. Press a piece of florist clay inside the lid and arrange the plastic figure and greenery in the clay. Squeeze a bead of white glue to the inside lip of the lid. (Or use a hot glue gun.)

Fill the jar with water and add about a teaspoon of silver glitter. Carefully place your scene inside the jar, sealing the lids tightly. Let dry overnight in the upside-down position. In the morning, shake the snow scene and watch "glittery" snow float down.

More Holiday Crafts!

Leaf

Berry

PAPER WREATH

Children will love to take this holly wreath home and hang it on the front door!

Cut the center from a paper plate. The outside rim will be the base for the wreath.

Carefully cut holly leaves from green paper. Overlap the leaves as you glue them to the rim. Glue red berries in bunches of three to the wreath. Add a real ribbon bow for a final touch.

SLEIGH DECORATION

This tiny sleigh can be used as a tree decoration or holiday favor.

Cut one section from a cardboard egg carton and trim to shape. Paint it a holiday color and add glitter if you like. Glue two pipe cleaners on the bottom for sleigh runners. Fill with candy and enjoy!

Movable Reindeer

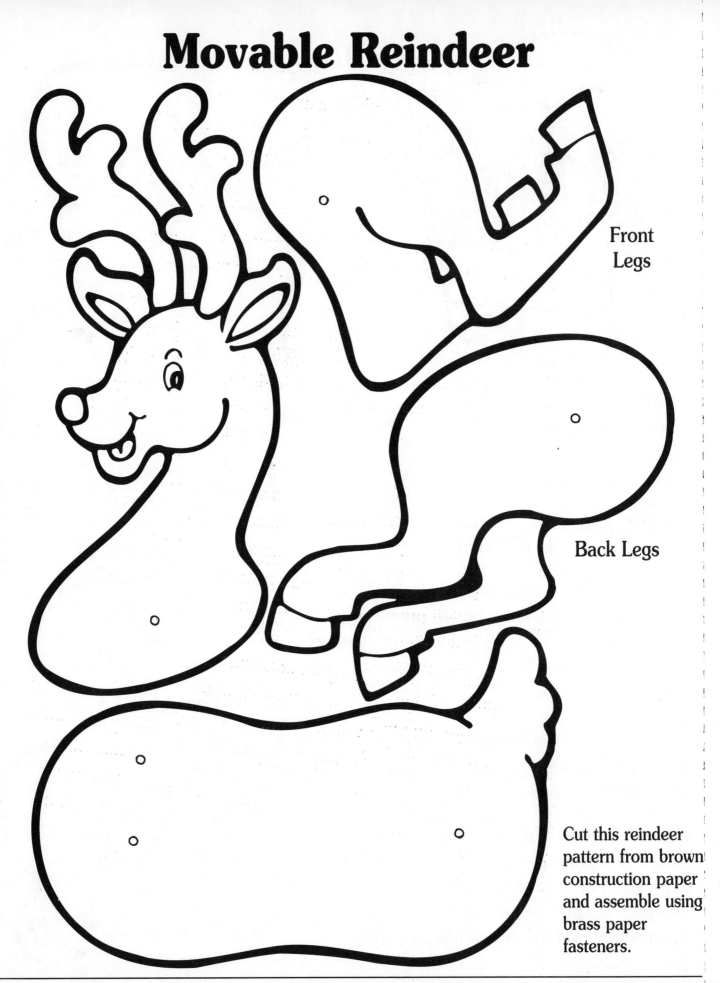

Front
Legs

Back Legs

Cut this reindeer
pattern from brown
construction paper
and assemble using
brass paper
fasteners.

56

Movable Santa

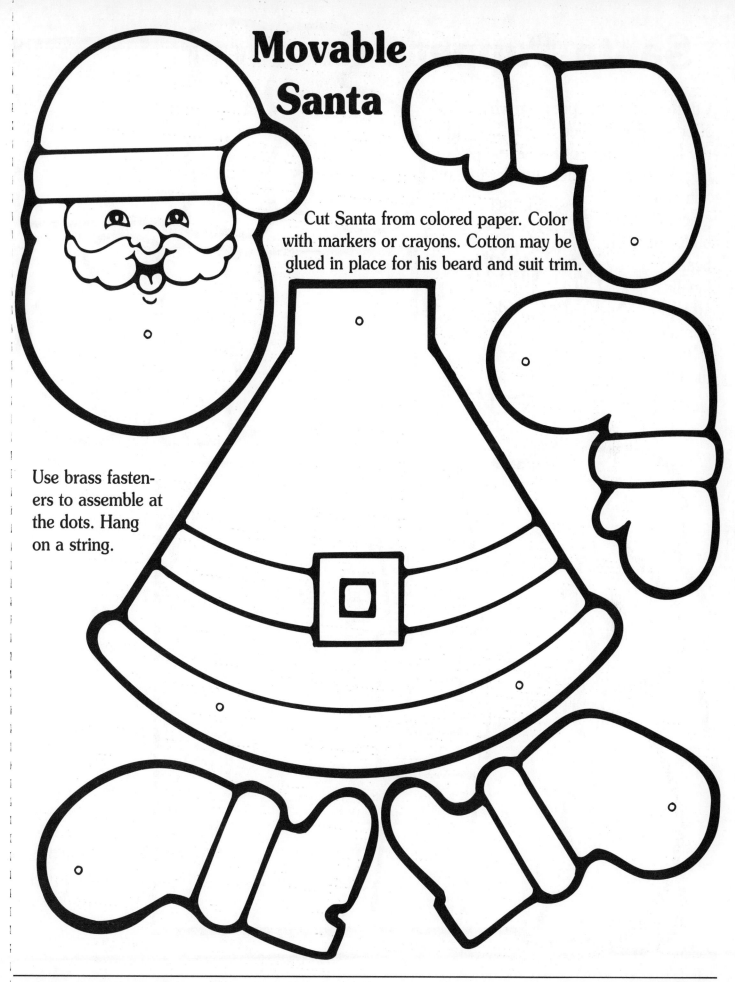

Cut Santa from colored paper. Color with markers or crayons. Cotton may be glued in place for his beard and suit trim.

Use brass fasteners to assemble at the dots. Hang on a string.

Santa Puppet

Cut this Santa puppet from white construction paper. Glue Santa's head to the folded bottom of a small paper bag. Place Santa's beard under the fold and glue in place. Glue his body under the beard. Finally, attach Santa's arms to the sides of the bag.

Santa
Puppet

TF1200 December Idea Book

Radical Reindeer

Have each student frame their holiday creative writing assignments in brown construction paper. Cut the reindeer patterns and four long strips from brown paper. Fan-fold the leg strips and assemble as shown. Children may like to write vocabulary words down the reindeer's legs.

Mouse
Topper

Color
and cut
this mouse pattern from grey, brown or white
construction paper. Place the mouse at the top of
your next creative writing paper. Glue the tail to the
bottom of your paper.

Stained Glass Holiday Bells

These "Stained Glass Pictures" are strikingly beautiful and wonderfully simple to make!

You will need the following materials:

Plastic food-storage wrap   Aluminum foil

Black construction paper   Tape

8" paper plates or cardboard circles

Permanent colored markers (red, green, yellow and black)

Stained Glass Holiday Tree

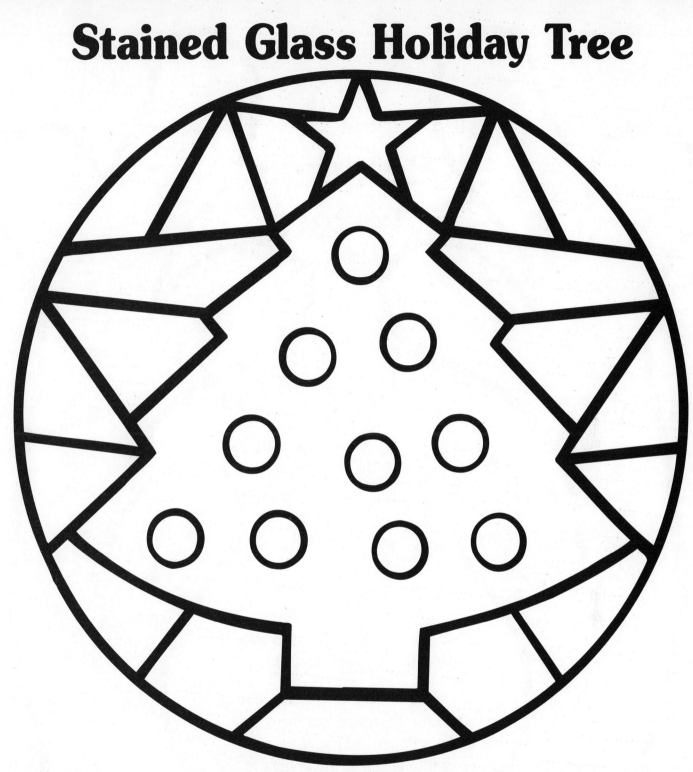

Tape the patterns to a smooth desk top. Ask each child to stretch a piece of plastic wrap over the pattern of his or her choice and tape in place. The child colors the picture using red, green and yellow markers. When the picture is completed, ask the student to trace all of the black lines using the black marker.

Next, have the student take a square of foil, (measuring about one foot) and crumple it carefully. He or she then spreads the foil over a paper plate, taping it in place. Finally, the student takes the finished stained glass picture and tapes it over the foil. Mount the entire project on black construction paper and hang in a window or display on the class bulletin board.

Reindeer Antlers

Children will be delighted to wear these cute "Reindeer Antlers."

Trace the antlers onto brown construction paper and cut them out. Make a paper headband for each student and staple the antlers to the sides as shown.

Christmas Tree Puppet

Paste the tree patterns to a small paper bag. Children can decorate their tree any way that they wish.

Holiday Cards

Place the dotted line along the folded edge of paper and cut out.

This gingerbread man pattern can be used in a variety of ways. Here are a few ideas:

1. Use the pattern as a holiday greeting card.

2. Make a gingerbread man booklet cover. Students can write holiday stories or creative gingerbread recipes.

Gingerbread Man

3. Use the pattern to make large gingerbread men ornaments.

4. Have each student cut and color their own gingerbread man. Line them up (hand to hand) across the class bulletin board.

Children love the story of the Gingerbread Man. You might like to read this rendition to your students.

The Story of the Gingerbread Man

Once upon a time, in a town not far away, the wife of Farmer Jack was busy in her kitchen.

It was the farmer's birthday and his wife was baking him something very special, a Gingerbread Man! He had raisins for eyes, a cherry for his nose and four candy gumdrops down his front for buttons. She also decorated him with wonderful frosting and gave him an extra big smile!

When she was satisfied that he was the best gingerbread man anyone could make, she put him on the window sill to cool while she finished cleaning up. As soon as she had turned her back, the Gingerbread Man jumped down from the window and out into the yard.

The farmer's wife saw him and shouted, "Stop, stop!" And Farmer Jack saw him and yelled, "Stop, stop!"

But the Gingerbread Man only laughed and sang, "Run, run, run as fast as you can. You'll never catch me. I'm the Gingerbread Man!"

Out of the yard he ran and down the road with the Farmer and his wife close behind. A local peddler was resting under a tree. When he saw the Gingerbread Man and the Farmer and his wife, he called, "Stop, stop!" But the Gingerbread Man didn't stop.

The Ginderbread Man kept running and yelled, "Run, run, run as fast as you can. You'll never catch me. I'm the Gingerbread Man! I ran away from Farmer Jack and his wife, and I can run away from you, I can, I can!" And away he ran, with all three of them close behind.

Soon they met the town's sheriff out for a ride on his horse. When the sheriff saw the Gingerbread Man, he shouted, "Stop, stop!"

But the Gingerbread Man only laughed and sang, "Run, run, run as fast as you can. You'll never catch me. I'm the Gingerbread Man! I ran away from Farmer Jack and his wife and the funny old Peddler and I can run away from you, I can, I can!" With that, he even ran faster! So the Sheriff joined in the chase.

Soon they passed the School Teacher and the Stable Owner out for a country stroll. "Stop, stop!" they yelled when they saw the Gingerbread Man.

But the Gingerbread Man only laughed and sang, "Run, run, run as fast as you can. You'll never catch me. I'm the Gingerbread Man! I ran away from Farmer Jack and his wife and the funny old Peddler and the Sheriff and his horse and I can run away from you, I can, I can!" Now, he really ran fast with everyone close behind.

Soon the Gingerbread Man came to a lake where a Wolf was sunning himself beside the water's edge. He saw the Gingerbread Man and he saw the School Teacher and Stable Owner and the Sheriff and his horse and the Peddler and Farmer Jack and his wife all chasing him.

"Jump on my back, Gingerbread Man, and I'll take you across the lake so those greedy people can't eat you," he said.

So the Gingerbread Man jumped on his back and the Wolf started swimming across the lake.

"Wolf, Wolf, my feet are getting wet!" the Gingerbread Man said.

"Then, jump on my shoulder," said the Wolf.

"Wolf, Wolf, I'm still getting wet!" exclaimed the Gingerbread Man.

"Then, jump on my nose," said the Wolf.

So the Gingerbread Man jumped on the Wolf's nose. Quick as a flash, the Wolf gobbled the Gingerbread Man up and ate him right down.

Which is exactly what should happen to all Gingerbread Men!

Try some of these Gingerbread Man activities in your classroom.

- Tell the story by substituting the characters' names with the names of some of your students.

- Have your students act out the story of the Gingerbread Man. They might even like to wear costumes and make props.

- Ask your class to discuss alternative choices that the Gingerbread Man could have made. How might he have saved himself from being eaten?

- Ask your students to write their own versions of the story of the Gingerbread Man. (They could have a futuristic setting or change the main characters. They might even like to change the entire ending of the story.)

GINGERBREAD MEN ORNAMENTS

Make simple paper gingerbread men ornaments from brown construction paper or heavy grocery bags. Trace the pattern and cut out. Decorate with white poster paint or colored markers. Add a dash of powdered cinnamon or ginger, applied with a small amount of glue, to your gingerbread man. This will make him smell like the real thing. Attach a thread to the top of his head and hang on the Christmas tree.

A fabric version of the same gingerbread man can be made by using two cloth cut-outs. Glue or stitch the two patterns together leaving a small opening. Stuff him with a small amount of polyester batting or cotton balls sprinkled with spices. Add a real ribbon or rickrack to decorate.

Movable Gingerbread Man

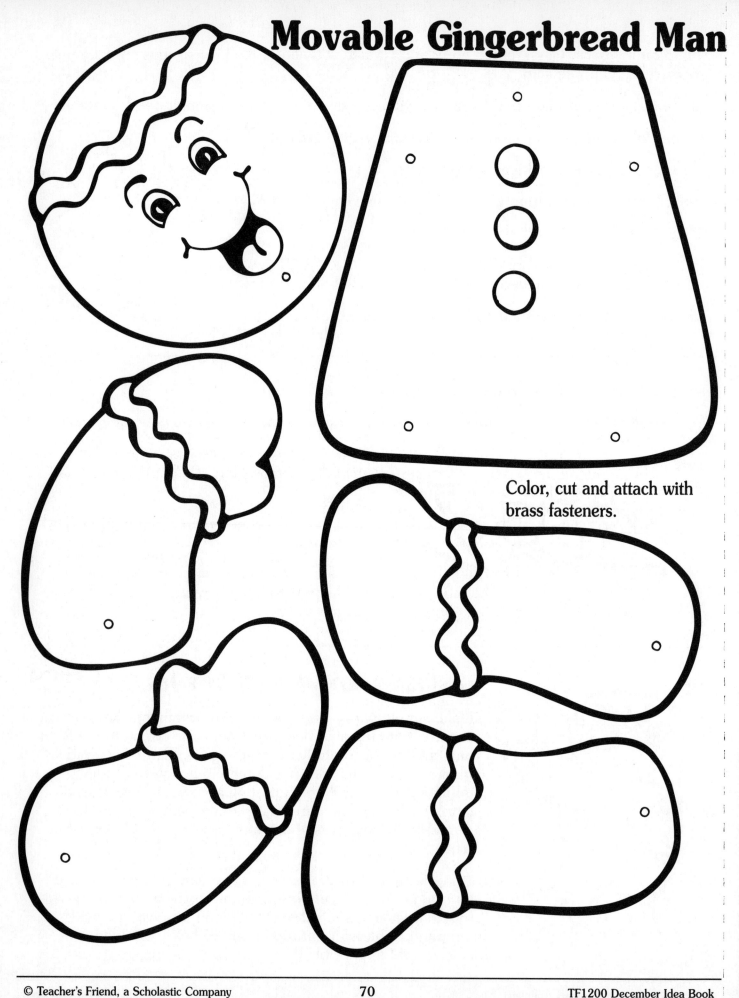

Color, cut and attach with brass fasteners.

Merry Christmas, Many Ways!

International Greetings

ACTIVITY 3

Learn to say "Merry Christmas" in another language!

BELGIUM	Zalig Kerstfeest	FRANCE	Joyeux Noel
CHINA	Shen Tan Kuai Loh	ENGLAND	Happy Christmas
SWEDEN	Gud Jul	GERMANY	Froehliche Weihnachten
RUSSIA	Kristos Razdajetsja	MEXICO	Feliz Navidad
DENMARK	Glaedelig Jul	ITALY	Guon Natale
PORTUGAL	Boas Festas	THE NETHERLANDS	Hartlijke Kerstroeten
POLAND	Boze Narodzenie	ROMANIA	Sarbatori Vesele
FINLAND	Hauskaa Joulua	IRELAND	Nodlaig Mhaith Chugnat

FIND THE NAMES OF ALL THE COUNTRIES IN THE PUZZLE BELOW.

```
K F T H P O R T U G A L U Y G F I N L A N D A
I V C X O R T M S W F T G B V C X D S F R T I
T D V B L D R U S S I A D R R U M A N I A X R
A D E R A H G T W A S D F G H J U K L I U Y E
L F V G N S E T E F G H Y U C H I N A V C X L
Y W Q A D X S W D E D C V F R T G B N H Y J A
D C V B N H Y H E H Y J U F I L O P M N H U N
L M K J H N Y U N E T H E R L A N D S E V T D
A S C X Z D R F O G Y H H A K T I U R F B H N
G E R M A N Y Y R G Y H J N H I N A T H Y U K
S C V E D T Y T X Y U J I C Y U J K L M N J G
D E R X R T Y H Z R T G Y E D E N M A R K U Y
D F G I G T H T Y H U J K L O I L M J R E S C
Z C B C S E N G L A N D F R T H N M K L O P O
X C Z O J U H N B G T V D C F F B E L G I U M
F G H B V C D R T Y U I P O L M X S W Q E R T
```

International Christmas Tree

Wish everyone a Merry Christmas with this "International Christmas Tree." Simply enlarge the tree to bulletin board size. Write holiday greetings in different languages on each ornament.

Feliz Navidad

God Jul

Zalig Kerstfeest

Sarbatori Vesele

Froehliche Weihnachten

Noel

Boze Norodzenie

Guon Natale

Hristos Razdajetsia

Nodlaig Mhaith Chugnat

Glaedelig Jul

Hauskaa Joulua

Hartlijke Kerstroeten

Shen Tan Kuai Loh

Happy Christmas

Boas Festas

TF1200 December Idea Book

Customs and Traditions

GREEN, WHITE & RED

The brilliant colors of green, red and white are traditional Christmas colors. We use them to decorate our home during the holidays and wrap our packages and gifts.

Legend tells us of a little lamb who made his journey to Bethlehem to see the Christ Child. On his way, his snowy white fleece became caught on a thorny holly bush. In his struggle to get free, his skin was pricked and tiny droplets of blood froze as red berries to the branches.

Most people believe, however, that the colors come from the richness of the evergreens, the snowy whiteness of the fields in winter, and the red crimson berries of the holly plant. Like many other aspects of Christmas, these merry colors brighten our mood during this hustle-bustle time of year.

(Ask children to draw a picture of a Christmas tree and decorate it with their own chosen holiday colors.)

CHRISTMAS CARDS

In the year 1870, an Englishman by the name of J.C. Horsely designed a picture on a simple card with a holiday greeting and sent it to his friends. This was the very first Christmas card. Gradually, almost everyone sent Christmas cards. Many were very fancy with real lace trim and edges embossed with silver and gold. Today it is still a popular tradition to send cards to faraway family and friends. What a wonderful way to wish people the joys of the holiday season!

(Have the children in your class make special Christmas cards that they can give to patients at a nearby nursing home or hospital. They might like to deliver the cards in person.)

Customs and Traditions

CHRISTMAS TINSEL

Decorating the Christmas tree with shimmering tinsel is an age-old tradition. According to legend, a poor old woman was unable to provide decorations for her children's Christmas tree. But when she awoke on Christmas morning, she discovered that a spider had spun a magical silver web which covered the tree. Everyone who saw the tree marveled at its glimmering beauty.

Today, a touch of tinsel creates a magical quality all of its own. Like shimmering jewels, these silver strands brighten our hearts during the holiday season.

(After finding a spider web early in the morning, spray it gently with a small amount of white spray paint. Carefully lift the web off using a sheet of black construction paper. The web will adhere to the paper. Collect several and display them on the class bulletin board.)

MISTLETOE

Mistletoe is a plant found in ancient legends. The Greeks once believed that its evergreen leaves were a symbol of good luck. As years went by, the English ceremoniously cut the mistletoe that grew high in the trees and carried it home in large bundles. During the winter months, they hung it over their doors as a sign of good luck. Since only happiness could pass beneath the mistletoe, enemies would embrace and seal their peace with a kiss of friendship. This is probably where today's custom originated that anyone caught beneath the mistletoe must be kissed.

(Bring some mistletoe to class to show your students. Please explain to them that the mistletoe berries are very poisonous and should never be put in the mouth.)

Customs and Traditions

REINDEER

Children are fascinated by Santa's flying reindeer. Explain to them that reindeer don't really fly and encourage students to find out some facts about actual reindeer. Here are some facts to get you started:

1. Another name for reindeer is caribou.
2. Although most reindeer are found in northern Scandinavia, they can also be found in Asia and North America.
3. The Lapps have trained reindeer to pull sleighs. They also use reindeer skin for clothing and boots. Reindeer milk and meat are commonly a part of the Lapps' diet.
4. Adult reindeer can grow to be 4 feet high and weigh up to 400 pounds.
5. The natural enemies of reindeer are wolves, lynxes and grizzly bears (not to mention humans).
6. Reindeer have larger antlers and hooves than other types of deer.
7. Female reindeer are the only type of female deer that have antlers.

GINGERBREAD

Throughout England and many other countries in Europe, gingerbread and gingerbread cookies are a family tradition. Shopkeepers and market vendors often sell these delicious molasses cookies throughout the year. In some areas you may even find Gingerbread Fairs where town people compete in making gingerbread houses and cookies.

Here in the United States, two towns in Pennsylvania hold similar celebrations. In February, the people of Wash Crossing, Pennsylvania celebrate "Gingerbread Days" with much sampling and selling of various gingerbread baked goods. Not far away, during the month of December, the entire town of Lahaska celebrates the Christmas holiday with a "Gingerbread House Competition." Numerous cash prizes are given to the most elaborately decorated gingerbread houses.

(Make gingerbread cookies in the classroom or bring in store-bought gingerbread cookies for your students to sample.)

Customs and Traditions

FIRST CHRISTMAS TREE

On Christmas Eve in Germany in 1605, a man by the name of Martin Luther was inspired by the overwhelming beauty of the night sky. The heavenly stars appeared to float down and rest on the branches of a wonderful fir tree. Because Luther wanted to share this magical moment with his family, he cut down the small tree and took it home. There, he decorated it with lighted candles. His family rejoiced as they gathered around the first Christmas tree.

Throughout the years, this custom has spread world-wide. With its festive colored lights and shiny glass balls, the Christmas tree has become a most special holiday tradition Even a tiny tree that has only a few decorations will always symbolize the love that first Christmas tree did so long ago.

(Your students might like to plant a fir tree on the school grounds, or perhaps donate a living Christmas tree to a needy family.)

CHRISTMAS GIFTS

Ever since the Three Wise Men placed their treasures before the Christ Child in Bethlehem, Christmas has been a time of giving gifts.

Through the years, countries around the world have established their own legends and customs of giving gifts at Christmas. In England, Father Christmas brings gifts to family members. In Holland, it's Sinterklaas and in Italy it is La Befana.

Today, this wonderful tradition of giving still touches our hearts in a special way. It is not difficult to look beyond the colorful ribbons and bright paper to feel the same spirit of giving as on that very first Christmas. After all, the most precious gift is the gift of love!

(Ask the children to write about a special gift that they would like to give someone that money cannot buy, a gift of love!)

"Peace on Earth"

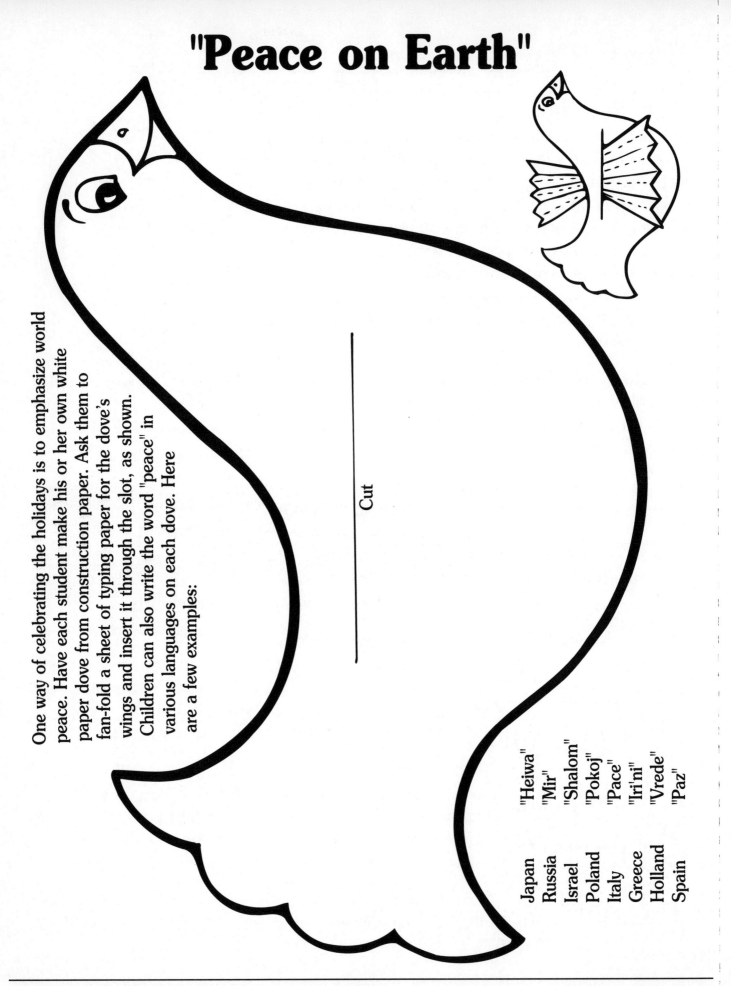

One way of celebrating the holidays is to emphasize world peace. Have each student make his or her own white paper dove from construction paper. Ask them to fan-fold a sheet of typing paper for the dove's wings and insert it through the slot, as shown. Children can also write the word "peace" in various languages on each dove. Here are a few examples:

Cut

Japan	"Heiwa"
Russia	"Mir"
Israel	"Shalom"
Poland	"Pokoj"
Italy	"Pace"
Greece	"Iri'ni"
Holland	"Vrede"
Spain	"Paz"

Dove of Peace

Color and cut out this lovely "Dove of Peace" pattern. Fold at the dotted line in the center and fold out each wing. Hang on a thread for a beautiful tree ornament or write your own holiday greeting and give as a card.

TF1200 December Idea Book

Creative Writing Page

Christmas in Mexico!

"Las Posadas"

Feliz Navidad Word Find

ACTIVITY 4

FIND THESE WORDS ASSOCIATED WITH CHRISTMAS IN MEXICO:

CHRISTMAS, MEXICO, PIÑATA, POSADAS, NAVIDAD, JOSEPH,
MARY, CHRIST CHILD, BETHLEHEM, STABLE

```
N D F G H Y C H R I S T M A S G Y U I O P H J K
A S D F G T Y U I K L O P M J K U I L O J M K L
V S D F G H M A R Y B H U K I O L P J H Y U I P
I S D F R T G H Y U J K I L O P M N O G T Y H N
D F G T H Y U J K I O M N V B N H Y S E R T Y U
A S D B E T H L E H E M G T Y U J H E S W E R T
D F G T Y G H U I K O P K L K I O M P F R T M A
S D F R T Y H U J K I O L M N B V D H F R T E R
P O S A D A S D R T Y U I O K J H B N M H U X D
Z X C F R T Y G B V F C D S W A X C G H J U I G
A S D F R T G Y H C H R I S T C H I L D H U C S
A X C F R T S T A B L E F T Y U H J K I N K O L
A X Z C V B H U J K L M N B V C X Z S E R T Y U
A X D R T Y H B N J I K L O P M N B G T R F V X
Z X S D C V F G B N H J U J K I P I Ñ A T A W E
R T Y U H G F D S W Q A X C V B N J K L O F D T
```

"FELIZ NAVIDAD" BULLETIN BOARD

Celebrate "Feliz Navidad" with this festive bulletin board.

Cut a large bird or animal shape from stiff poster board for the piñata. Cover with pieces of colorful tissue-paper squares and streamers. Pin it to the board with the heading "Feliz Navidad!" Post students' stories about "Las Posadas" around the piñata.

You might like to save the piñata for future use during Cinco de Mayo or Mexico Independence Day.

THE CHRISTMAS STORY
(From the book of <u>Luke</u> in the Bible)

And it came to pass in those days that there went out a decree from Caesar Augustus that all the world should be taxed.

And Joseph also went up from Galilee, out of the city of Nazareth, into Judaea, unto the city of David, which is called Bethlehem; (because he was of the house and lineage of David)

To be taxed with Mary, his espoused wife, being great with child.

And so it was that, while they were there, the days were accomplished that she should be delivered.

And she brought forth her firstborn son, and wrapped him in swaddling clothes and laid him in a manger, because there was no room for them in the inn.

And there were in the same country shepherds abiding in the field, keeping watch over their flock by night.

And, lo, the angel of the Lord came upon them, and the glory of the Lord shone round about them and they were sore afraid.

And the angel said unto them, "Fear not; for behold, I bring you good tidings of great joy, which shall be to all people.

For unto you is born this day in the city of David a Saviour, which is Christ the Lord..."

And suddenly there was with the angel a multitude of the heavenly host praising God and saying,

"Glory to God in the highest, and on earth peace, good will toward men."

CHRISTMAS IN MEXICO

In Mexico, the most cherished custom of Christmas is the Posadas. Posadas, meaning lodging, is the name given to the nine days of celebration before "La Navidad," Christmas Day. This celebration commemorates the journey of Mary and Joseph to Bethlehem and their search for lodging each night.

In the countryside, children gather at private homes. Each child is provided with a candle, which is lit as the children form a line and slowly begin to parade down the streets. At the head of this procession, two children carry small figures of the Holy Family. As they approach each house, they are turned away until they arrive at the replica of the stable in Bethlehem. There they arrange the figures, placing the Christ Child in the manger, exactly at midnight.

After prayers before the créche, there is merrymaking and the breaking of the piñata. Children scramble for the gifts and candy that spill from inside the piñata. Fireworks are then set off in celebration.

Children receive their gifts on January 6 instead of Christmas Day. This day is known as the "Day of the Wise Men." Instead of hanging up their stockings, children put their shoes out for the Wise Men to fill with toys.

Las Posadas Crafts

LAS POSADAS CANDLE

Children can each make their own candle for the Posadas procession using these simple directions.

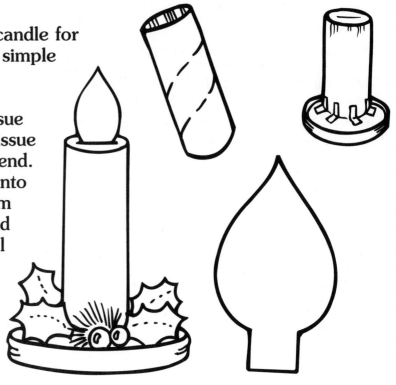

Have each student cover a toilet tissue tube with a large sheet of colorful tissue paper, making sure they cover one end. Tell them to tuck the excess paper into the open end of the tube. Have them tape the tube to a painted jar lid and decorate it with paper holly or small plastic holiday greenery. Cut the flame pattern from yellow construction paper and insert it into a slit that has been cut in the covered top of the tube. Use the candles as holiday decorations or let your students carry their candles in the Posadas procession.

MINIATURE PIÑATA

Make a miniature piñata to use as a Christmas tree decoration!

You will need:

styrofoam egg cartons	yarn
felt pens or paint	tissue paper
wrapped candy pieces	glue and scissors

Cut an egg cup from your carton and trim the edges. Decorate as you wish. Push a piece of yarn through the top for hanging. Cut two 3" x 6" strips of tissue paper. Clip the bottom edge to make a fringe. Glue the tip of the strips to the inside edge of your cup. Fasten a wrapped piece of candy to the inside of the piñata with tape.

There you have it! A perfect miniature piñata to hang on the tree or give as a gift!

Nativity

Children can color and cut out these nativity patterns. Have each child paste the scene onto a sheet of construction paper.

Mexico

Creative Writing Page

Christmas in Italy!

CHRISTMAS IN ITALY

Several days before Christmas, the children of Italy go door to door singing favorite Christmas carols. They are often accompanied by pipers wearing bright red jackets and broad-brimmed hats with red tassels. The pipers carry bagpipes, flutes and oboes, on which they play sweet holiday music. Often the children and pipers are invited into homes to sing old carols and folk songs.

On Christmas Eve, many candles are lit as the children in the family take turns telling the wonderful story of Christmas and the birth of the holy "Bambino." At this time, Italian families gather around their beloved "Presepio," a shrine to the Holy Child, and pray. After a 24-hour fast, all members of the family then sit down to a feast of delicious lasagna and spaghetti.

On the twelfth day of the holidays, January 6, a kindly old witch known as "La Befana" brings gifts to the children. Legend has it that when Christ was born, the shepherds told La Befana of the wondrous happenings and of the guiding star, but she delayed setting out. Every Christmas since, she has wandered in search of the Holy Child, leaving gifts at each home in hope of finding Him inside.

La Befana is often shown as being old and ugly, but the children of Italy love her very much. That is, unless they have been naughty, for then she will fill their shoes with coal and ashes instead of candy and gifts.

EASY MINI PIZZAS

In celebration of Christmas in Italy, have each child make their own mini pizza!

Give each student one half of an English muffin. Spoon 1 tablespoon prepared pizza sauce on top and add grated cheese. Pepperoni or sliced olives can also be added. Bake in a conventional or microwave oven until the cheese bubbles.

Children will love experiencing this little taste of Italy during the holidays!

La Befana

Cut this cute "La Befana" witch from construction paper and assemble as shown. (You may want to use red or green paper for her dress and hat.) Attach a string to the top of her hat and hang on the tree.

1.

2.

3.

4.

Cut out

Italy

Holiday Wreath

FOLD

The Christmas wreath probably originated in ancient Rome where the people hung decorative wreaths as a sign of victory and celebration. Wreaths made of evergreens represent eternal life.

Have students decorate this wreath booklet pattern and write their own Christmas story inside.

La Befana Puppet

Make this paper bag puppet and let children act out the story of La Befana.

Creative Writing Page

Christmas in Holland!

SINTERKLAAS DAY - DECEMBER 6TH

During the last weekend in November, "Sinterklaas" (Santa Clause) arrives in Holland on a large steamboat from his home in Spain. Along with him he brings his white horse and dozens of helpers, "Zwarte Piets" (Black Peters). They accompany Sinterklaas to Amsterdam, where large crowds come out to greet him in person.

During the weeks before Sinterklaas Day, small children try to be very good. If they are naughty, Zwarte Piet may swat them with a birch stick or, worse yet, take them away to Spain in his big bag. During this time, adults and older children are busy preparing surprise gifts for the family. The presents are wrapped in funny, unusual ways with special notes written in verse. These gifts are then hidden away until Sinterklaas Day.

The night before Sinterklaas Day, children place their wooden shoes by the fireplace, which are filled with carrots or hay for Sinterklaas' white horse. In the morning, they hope these things will be replaced with gifts from Sinterklaas. In some homes, the doorbell rings and a Piet's hand will throw candies and cookies into the room, quickly slamming the door behind him. Children run to gather the sweets while Mother pulls in a large basket of gifts left outside. In other homes, gifts are not opened until little children have gone to bed. Then the rest of the family will open presents and read the attached poems signed by "Sinterklaas."

A traditional holiday sweet in Holland is marzipan, which is an almond paste candy shaped into funny things such as animals or fruit. Initials of pure chocolate are also a favorite treat.

As you can see, Sinterklaas Day is a very happy time with festive celebrations and much merrymaking. Christmas Day, however, is celebrated in a very quiet way with family get-togethers and church services.

WRITE THESE WORDS ON THE CLASS-ROOM CHALKBOARD AND ASK STUDENTS TO WRITE THEIR OWN STORIES ABOUT "SINTERKLAAS."

Holland	Spain
Sinterklaas	White Horse
Zwarte Piet	Wooden Shoe
Steamboat	Gifts

TF1200 December Idea Book

Wooden Shoe

Name

Mount wooden shoes on a bulletin board. Children can cut out and color the carrot and oats and place them in the shoe.

After December 6, have students replace the shoes with pictures of presents brought by Sinterklaas.

Holland
Netherlands

Holland
Netherlands

TF1200 December Idea Book

Windmill Ornament

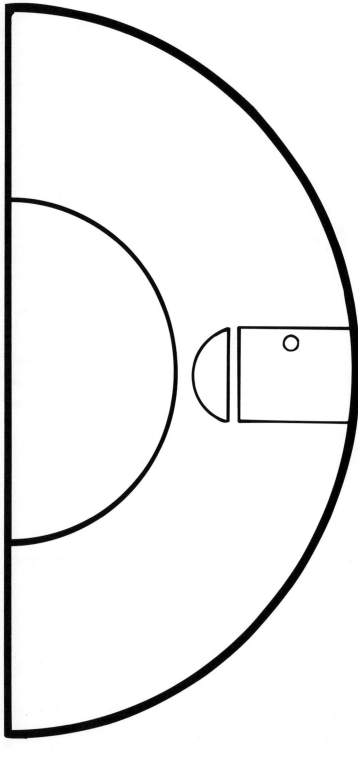

Children will love making Dutch windmills as tree decorations.

Color and cut out the two windmill pieces. Form the half-circle into the shape of a cone and tape in place. Attach the blades with a brass paper fastener as shown in the illustration.

Add a string to the top and hang on the tree.

POEMS FROM SINTERKLAAS

On Sinterklaas Day, December 6, families in Holland have a great deal of fun playing tricks on one another.

You might create a classroom treasure hunt where one clue leads to other clues hidden all over the classroom. The "treasure" (a bag of cookies or other treats) should be hidden in a clever place for students to find at the at the end of the search.

As a creative writing activity, have students write funny poems to each other as they do in Holland. Have children draw names so that no one is left out. Each poem should be addressed to an individual child and signed by "Sinterklaas!" (Remember to emphasize that only "nice" poems will be accepted.)

Children can take turns reading their "Sinterklaas notes" to the rest of the class.

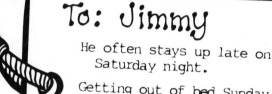

To: Cindy

She's the best speller. She really is good!
If only she'd spell the words should, would and could!

Sinterklaas

To: Jimmy

He often stays up late on Saturday night.

Getting out of bed Sunday takes all of his might!

Sinterklaas

DUTCH TREAT

Create a real "Dutch Treat" in the classroom with this special windmill.

Mount the paper windmill onto the class bulletin board. Cut the blades from heavy poster board and attach them to the center with straight pins. The windmill blades should be turned periodically to direct children to particular center activities.

Windmill Booklet

Have each student make this booklet cover from construction paper. The windmill blades can also be cut from construction paper and attached to the windmill with a brass fastener. The titles of creative stories can be written on the blades.

Creative Writing Page

Christmas in Sweden!

Santa Lucia Day

CHRISTMAS IN SWEDEN - DECEMBER 13TH

On one of the shortest days of the year, Sweden celebrates the feast of Santa Lucia. Dressed in a white gown and wearing a wreath of lighted candles on her head, the eldest daughter in each family, representing Santa Lucia, brings good will and light to the long winter's night. Early in the morning, she prepares sweet cakes and coffee for each member of the family while they are still in bed. She then wakens the family by singing the traditional song "Santa Lucia." On Christmas Eve, the houses are prepared for "Jultometen," Father Christmas, who arrives in a sleigh assisted by miniatures of himself. The tree is decorated with real lighted candles. At midnight, the story of the first Christmas is read aloud and gifts are opened. Christmas Day is very quiet, with church services in the morning and the rest of the day spent at home with the entire family.

SANTA LUCIA

Santa Lucia was a young girl that lived in Italy in the second century A.D. She was a very strong believer in the Christian religion, which was banned in her country at the time. Lucia thought that her family should give all of their wealth to the poor, but family members strongly disagreed with her.

One day her mother became very ill. Lucia persuaded her to make a journey to a Christian holy place. Lucia's mother was cured and in gratitude for this miracle she agreed to give away her wealth. Several days later, the government discovered that Lucia was a Christian and condemned her to death. Centuries later, in honor of her good deeds, Lucia was declared a saint by the church. Because the name Lucia means light, she became the saint of vision and light.

Although this story is several hundred years old, Santa Lucia Day was observed in only a few Swedish villages until recently. Members of these villages believed that Santa Lucia could be seen on her special day serving hot rolls and drinks to the poor.

Santa Lucia Day falls on one of the shortest days in the year, December 13. In Sweden, the winter nights are so long that in the far north the sun only shines for about one hour. What could be more cheerful than to honor Santa Lucia with this festival of light and goodwill?

Santa Lucia Headwreath

Every girl in class can become Santa Lucia for a day with this headwreath pattern.

Cut paper headbands for every girl in the class. Students can cut their own candles from yellow or white construction paper. Leaves can be cut from green paper. Fasten the candles and leaves to the headbands with glue or staples.

Fit the headwreath to the student's head and staple into place.

The girls may like to pass out cookies to the boys as they sing the old song, "Santa Lucia."

TF1200 December Idea Book

Sweden

TF1200 December Idea Book

Sweden

Swedish Desserts

SANTA LUCIA SWEET ROLLS

Ingredients: 5 cups of Bisquick
2 eggs
6 tablespoons cooking oil
3/4 cup milk

Combine the ingredients in the order given. Divide the dough so that each child has a piece. Ask the children to shape the dough into 8" long rolls and curl the ends to form an "S" shape. Add raisins to decorate if you wish. Bake on a greased cookie sheet at 375 degrees for about 15 minutes.

While the rolls are baking, prepare a frosting made with 1 1/2 cups powdered sugar and 5 teaspoons milk. While the rolls are still warm from the oven, brush with the frosting.

"JULGRÖT" - RICE PUDDING

Christmas dinner in Sweden includes a special dessert of rice pudding called "julgröt." It is customary to place an almond in the large bowl of pudding. Whoever gets the almond in their dish has good luck throughout the new year!

Serve your students rice pudding (complete with an almond) as a tasty way to celebrate the holidays.

"OUR BRIGHT LIGHTS"

This "bright" bulletin board idea will complement your studies of Santa Lucia.

Cut one candle and flame from construction paper for each child in class. Arrange on the bulletin board as shown. (Holly or other leaves across the bottom will add a nice touch.)

Award gold stars or stickers for all completed assignments. The children will love to place them on their own candles for classmates to see.

Advent Calendar Pictures

Children of Sweden enjoy using Advent Calendars! Ask students to paste this sheet onto a larger piece of construction paper and color the pictures. Also, have them color the fireplace on the next page. Ask a parent volunteer to cut out the "stone" windows using an art knife and fold each window on the dotted lines. Apply paste to the outer edges of the fireplace and position it on top of this page. Beginning December 1, children can open the windows as a count-down to Christmas.

Advent Calendar

Hanukkah!

"Festival of Lights"

THE STORY OF HANUKKAH

Hanukkah is a happy festival celebrated by the Jewish people. The holiday is honored for eight days beginning on the twenty-fifth day of the Hebrew month of Kislev falling within the month of November or December. Hanukkah commemorates the victory of the Maccabbes over the Syrians in 165 B.C.

The Jews of Palestine, under the leadership of Judas Maccabeus, successfully fought a war against King Antiochus. The King had forced all of his subjects to practice the religion of Greece, denying the Jews their religious freedom. During this time, Palestine was under Syrian-Greek rule. When the Maccabbes returned to their temple which had been previously occupied by the Greeks, they found only enough sacred oil to light the holy menorah for one day. By divine miracle, however, the lamp continued to burn for eight days. In celebration, the event was called the "Festival of Lights."

Today, Jewish families celebrate the Festival of Lights by lighting a special candelabra, called a *menorah*. The holiday begins the first day by lighting the first candle at sundown on the twenty-fourth of Kislev. A "servant" candle called Shammash is also lit each night and is used to light the other candles. Each evening an additional candle is burned until all eight candles are burning together. At this time, family members say blessings of thanks to God.

After lighting the Menorah, Jewish families play games and exchange gifts. Children especially like the holiday of Hanukkah. The ancient game using a four-sided top known as the dreydl is played and traditional holiday goodies such as "latkes," potato pancakes are served. The custom of gift-giving is also very special and has been included in Hanukkah celebrations for centuries.

THE DREYDL

A dreydl is a special four-sided top. The Hebrew letters "N", "G", "H", and "S" are written on the sides of the top. These letters stand for the words, "Nes", "Gadol", "Haya", and "Sham", which mean "a great miracle happened." Long ago, Jewish people were forbidden to come together and pray. In order to practice their religion, they pretended to play games with this little top. Here is how to play a game with the dreydl:

Assemble the dreydl pattern on page 118 according to the directions. Give ten dried beans to each player and place an empty bowl in the center of the table. Before each turn, every player must put a bean in the bowl. The players take turns spinning the top. If the letter "N" turns up, the player wins no beans; if "G" turns up he or she wins all of the beans in the bowl; if "H" turns up, he wins half of the beans in the bowl and if "S" turns up, he must put one bean in the bowl. The game continues until one player has won all of the beans.

Menorah

Cut out the menorah and candles. Add one candle for each day of Hanukkah.

FOLD

Dreydl Pattern

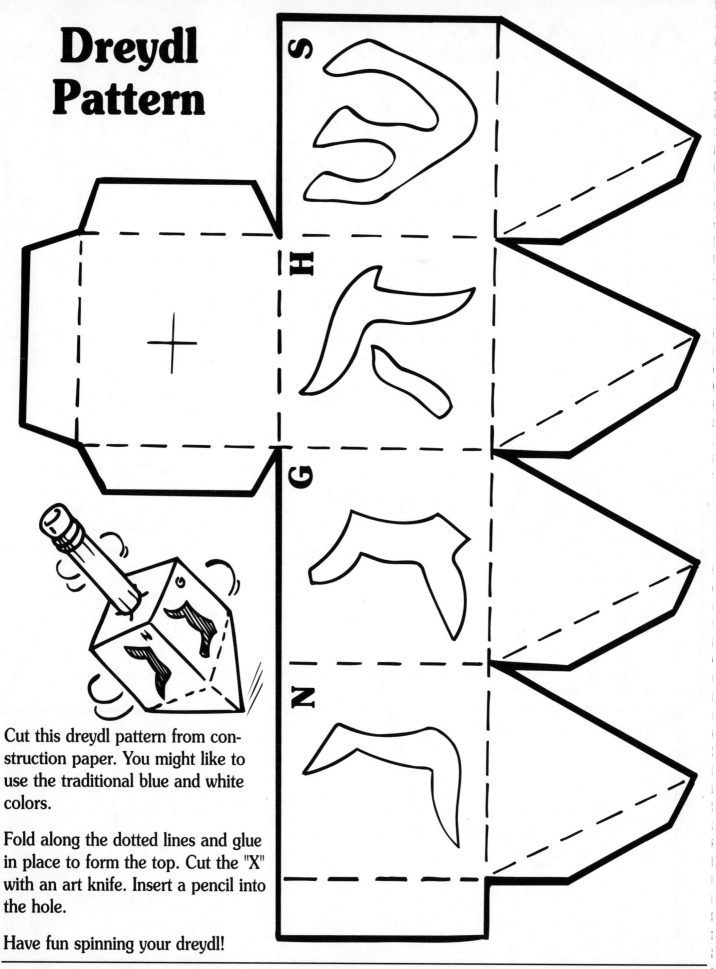

Cut this dreydl pattern from construction paper. You might like to use the traditional blue and white colors.

Fold along the dotted lines and glue in place to form the top. Cut the "X" with an art knife. Insert a pencil into the hole.

Have fun spinning your dreydl!

Hanukkah Booklet

Have students write their own stories or poems about Hanukkah using this booklet cover.

Display the booklets on the class bulletin board.

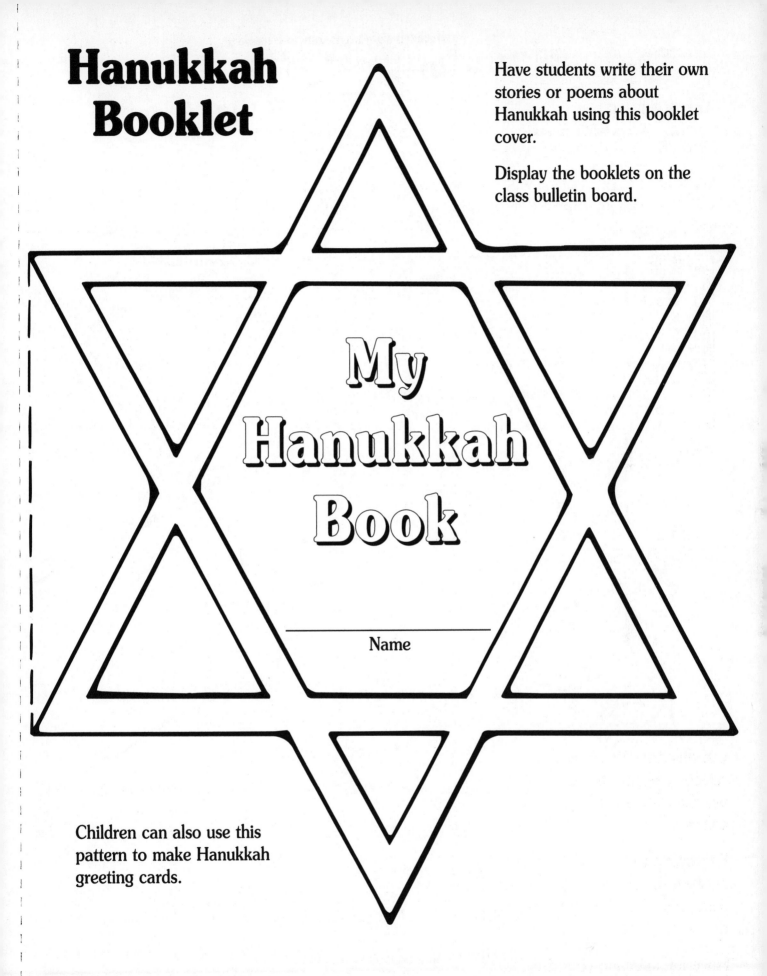

My Hanukkah Book

_____
Name

Children can also use this pattern to make Hanukkah greeting cards.

Hanukkah Word Find

ACTIVITY 5

FIND THESE HANUKKAH WORDS:

MACCABBES, DREYDL, JEWISH, MENORAH, HANUKKAH, EIGHT, CANDLES, GIFTS, LATKES, FESTIVAL, LIGHT, FAMILY, SHAMMASH, PRAYERS

```
B N M K J H A N U K K A H C B G F D T Y J K
J W R T Y U I O P K L J M N B G F D S F G Y
E W D F T G H Y T H Y U J S E R T X Z A I T
W S F R D R E Y D L S E M S E R F V X F F W
I E R D S C I G T H Y Y E D F C Y U I O T Q
S W E R T R G S E Y U I N D Q A T Y U O S M
H H A S E F H B V C S B O W X N U I O P L J
K J H G D E T W X V J K R N M D E Y U O P L
M A C C A B B E S L R T A R G L G H J U K I
A S D F R T Y H G F V B H J T E U I O P L N
A S W Q E L A T K E S F R E R S K L I G H T
X Z C V B N H Y T G F R E D S W Q M K L O P
S H A M M A S H Y B V F R E D C X S Y H K L
S E R T H J K I U Y N J P R A Y E R S G N M
W X C V G Y T R F B H U J K O P L M H Y T B
S E R F V D C T H F E S T I V A L R F G H J
S D F R T Y H J U I K L O P M B G T F V C D
A F A M I L Y E R F V G Y U J N H G B V D E
```

ACTIVITY 6

MATCH THESE FACTS ABOUT HANUKKAH

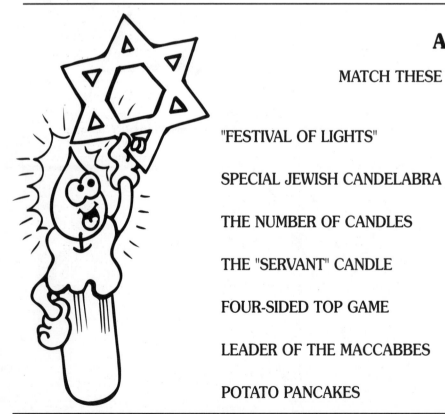

"FESTIVAL OF LIGHTS"   DREYDL

SPECIAL JEWISH CANDELABRA   MENORAH

THE NUMBER OF CANDLES   HANUKKAH

THE "SERVANT" CANDLE   JUDAS MACCABEUS

FOUR-SIDED TOP GAME   LATKES

LEADER OF THE MACCABBES   SHAMMASH

POTATO PANCAKES   EIGHT

"HAPPY HANUKKAH" BULLETIN BOARD

Create a festive Hanukkah bulletin board with this simple idea:

Use patterns cut into shapes of Hanukkah symbols. Have students trace the shapes onto construction paper. Ask them to write interesting facts or creative stories about this special Jewish holiday.

Mount the title "Happy Hanukkah" and display the new creations.

STAR OF DAVID

Fold one sheet of blue and two sheets of white construction paper in half. Place the star pattern along the fold and cut it out.

Insert a straight pin along the folds of the three cut stars as shown. Attach a loop of thread or string on which to hang your "Star of David."

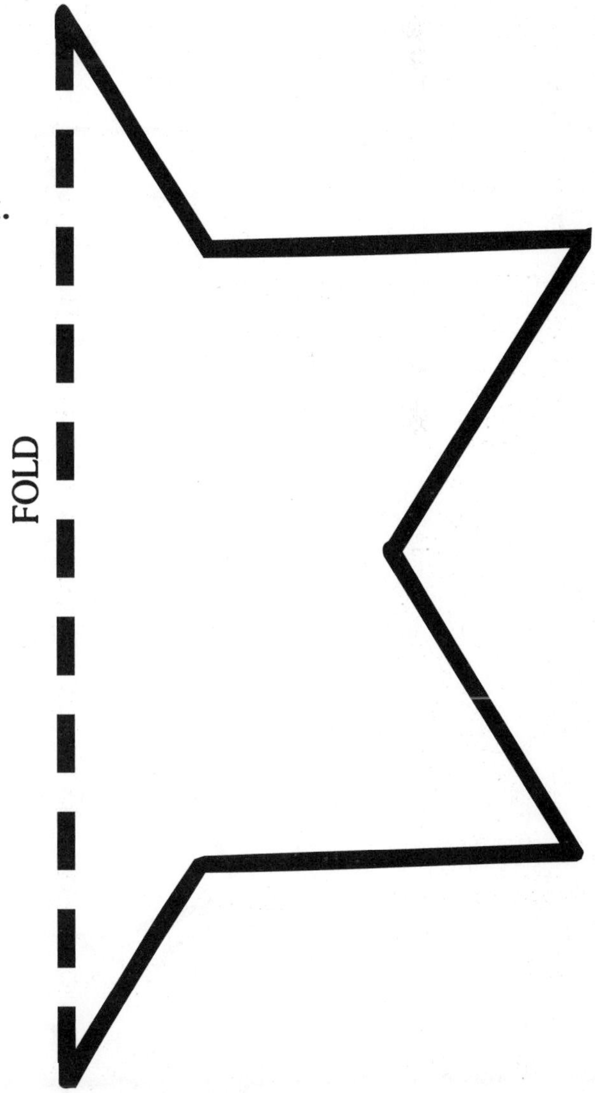

FOLD

Israel

Creative Writing Page

Kwanzaa!

"The First Fruits of the Harvest"

The Kwanzaa Holiday

Kwanzaa is a modern festival honoring the ancient African tradition of celebrating the year's harvest. The Swahili word Kwanzaa means "the first fruits of the harvest." This seven day holiday was started in 1966 by African-Americans in the United States. It is a special time for many African-American families to learn about the traditions and language of their African ancestors. On each day of the holiday, one of the seven principles of Kwanzaa is emphasized and a candle is lit in recognition. Members of the household wear brightly colored clothing that reflects the brilliant designs of African art and life. Kwanzaa is not meant to replace the holiday of Christmas, but rather a time to enrich cultural pride and cooperation.

KWANZAA SYMBOLS

mkeka - straw mat that represents a firm foundation. The muhindi and mazao are placed on the mat.

kinara - candle holder which holds seven candles.

mishumma - seven candles, each representing a principle of Kwanzaa. (One candle is black, three are green and three are red.)

muhindi - harvested corn that represents the hope of the future and the value of children to the family unit. One ear of corn is used to symbolize each child in the household.

mazao - various fruits and vegetables symbolizing the harvest and cooperation.

zawadi - simple gifts like books or hand-crafted items which are lovingly given to children.

kibombe cha umoja - this unity cup is passed to everyone taking part in the Kwanzaa celebration to symbolize the value of family and community.

Kinara
candleholder

KWANZAA

Color each candle the
appropriate color for
the days of Kwanzaa.

Principles of Kwanzaa

Day One
Umoja (Unity)
"We help each other."

Day Two
Kujichagulia (Self-Determination)
"We decide things for ourselves."

Day Three
Ujima (Collective Work)
"We work together to make life better."

Day Four
Ujamma (Cooperative Economics)
"We build and support our own businesses."

Day Five
Nia (Purpose)
"We have a reason for living."

Day Six
Kuumba (Creativity)
"We use our minds and hands to make things."

Day Seven
Imani (Faith)
"We believe in ourselves, our ancestors, and our future."

Display a large Kinara complete with seven candles (mishumma) on the class bulletin board. Enlarge the principles of Kwanzaa and pin one up each day of the celebration.

Muhindi Booklet Cover

Have each child make her or his own "Muhindi" booklet cover. Inside, they can write stories of how their families celebrate Kwanzaa.

FOLD

Display the "Muhindi" on the class board along with student-made, paper-woven mats and other symbols of Kwanzaa.

International
Children

Africa

Africa

131

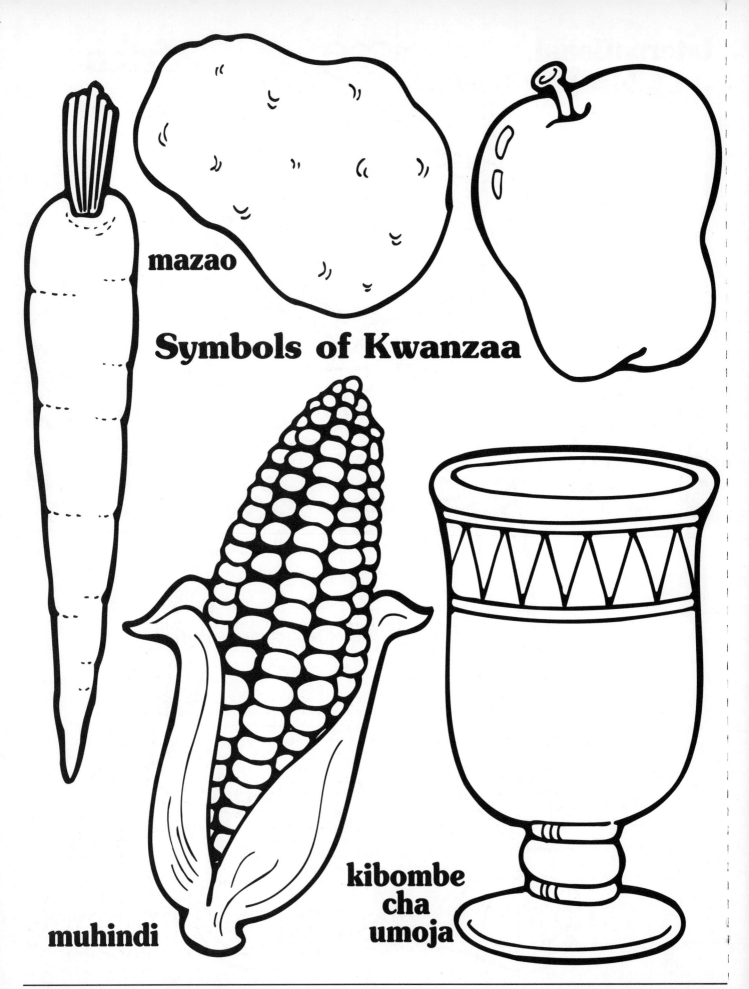

mazao

Symbols of Kwanzaa

muhindi

kibombe
cha
umoja

mishumma

zawadi

**Symbols
of
Kwanzaa**

mkeka

Creative Writing Page

Bulletin Boards and more!

Decembers Best!

Bulletin Boards and more...

HOLIDAYS IN OTHER LANDS Use the "International Children" in this book for a bulletin board idea that ties right in with your seasonal studies. Add a title and students' research papers to complete the board.

HOLIDAYS in OTHER LANDS

FIREPLACE IN THE CLASSROOM

To make this warm and cozy fireplace, cut red construction paper into 6" x 9" rectangles. Pin the rectangles to the class bulletin board as shown in the illustration to make the bricks. Cut one long strip of paper for the mantel and label with the teacher's name and grade. Write students' names on paper stockings and pin them to the mantel. Fill the stockings with take-home awards.

Let the children take the stockings home on the last day before vacation.

The stocking pattern can be found on page 49 of this December Idea Book.

Bulletin Boards and more...

PEACE ON EARTH

Mount a large map of the world on the class bulletin board or draw your own. Cut berries and holly leaves from construction paper and pin them to form a wreath around the map. Students can write papers about their solutions to world's problems.

HANDSOME CHRISTMAS TREE

Ask each student to trace and cut two handprints from green construction paper. Have them write their names in bold letters in the center of each handprint. Curl the fingers with a pencil. Pin the handprints to the class bulletin board as illustrated. This is a "handsome" way to make a class tree.

If you end up with too many handprints, you can make a wreath for the classroom door.

GIFT OF LOVE

A "Gift of Love" is one which money cannot buy.

Ask children to design holiday packages using real wrapping paper and ribbon. Have each student write a paper about a "gift of love" they would like to give. Display the papers on the board under each package. Visitors can flip up a corner of the package to read the students' papers.

Bulletin Boards and more...

CANDY CANE NAME DISPLAY

Children will love to see their names displayed on this cheery bulletin board.

Cut a large candy cane from poster board or butcher paper. Use red paint or markers to add the red stripes. Children can sign their own names, or you can do it for them. Large paper holly can announce your holiday greeting.

12 DAYS TILL CHRISTMAS

Green foil leaves and yellow paper pears comprise this clever holiday bulletin board.

Arrange the leaves and pears on a large, paper-cut tree pattern. Write the numbers one to twelve on the pears. Remove one pear each day as a count-down to Christmas vacation.

HOLIDAY'S BEST

Make these festive candles by displaying good work papers on 9" x 12" red construction paper. Attach a bright yellow paper flame to the top of each candle. Add the title "Holiday's Best" to the top of the board. Attach paper holly as a decoration to this easy to make bulletin board display.

Partridge and Pear Tree Patterns

TF1200 December Idea Book

Antler Pattern

Students may like to choose a name for their reindeer and write it on the antlers. They may choose the traditional names of Dasher and Dancer, etc., or make up their own.

The reindeer can also be used in a bulletin board display with students' names written on each one.

Jeffrey

Name

Reindeer Pattern

Nose

Have each student cut this reindeer pattern from construction paper and color with crayons.

Santa Sign Man

Enlarge this Santa pattern onto poster-board. Cut out and color.

Display him on the class bulletin board as illustrated.

TF1200 December Idea Book

Answer Key

ACTIVITY 1

UNSCRAMBLE SANTA'S REINDEER NAMES.

ZNETILB	B L I T Z E N
PDIUC	C U P I D
XINVE	V I X E N
HSREAD	D A S H E R
MOTEC	C O M E T
CANDRE	D A N C E R
DULOHPR	R U D O L P H
CRNEARP	P R A N C E R
DDNORE	D O N D E R

ACTIVITY 2

```
L K I J H O P L L L M N B V C S T A R H N J K O P
W C V G H J B O W S S D F G Y T R E D F V B N M K
S D R T G F H R Y N J H U I K D E R T I G T Y H J
G G T Y H J U N R E W Q R T Y U I K L C D R T Y U
A D E R T H C A N D Y C A N E S K L J I D F T F G
R F T Y J G H M N B Y N A L R U D R T C F G Y U M
L F G T H Y N E J K R E W X Z A N G E L M J G Y R
A D E R T Y H N D F B C F R T Y H J H E J N H M K
N F T F T G H T I N S E L B H J U I L S D R T S X
D F G T H Y U S K I L O J E F T G H U J N B V C X
P I N E C O N E S T Y H N L G Y U I P R E W D S F
B G H U Y T F G H J U I K L G V B N M K L P O I U
S E R T H J U I O K J M N S E D C V B N M K J U Y
S E R T G F V B H J K L I G H T S E W R T F G H J
A S D C V B N M K J H G F D S A T R E W Y U I O P
R F D E S W Q A Z X C V B N G Y T U I J K L O P U
```

ACTIVITY 3

```
K F T H P O R T U G A L U Y G F I N L A N D A
I V C X O R T M S W F T G B V C X D S F R T L
T D V B L D R U S S I A D R R U M A N I A X I
A D E R A H G T W A S D F G H J U K L I U Y E
L F V G N S E T E F G H Y U C H I N A V C X L
Y W Q A D X S W D E D C V F R T G B N H Y J A
D C V B N H Y H E H Y J U F I L O P M N H U N
L M K J H N Y U N E T H E R L A N D S E V T D
A S C X Z D R F O G Y H H A K T I U R F B H N
G E R M A N Y Y R G Y H J N H I N A T H Y U K
S C V E D T Y T X Y U J I C Y U J K L M N J G
D E R X R T Y H Z R T G Y E D E N M A R K U Y
D F G I G T H T Y H U J K L O I L M J R E S C
Z C B C O J U H G B T V D C F F B E L G I U M
X C Z J H J B V C D R T Y U I P O L M X S W Q E R T
F G H B V C D R T Y U I P O L M X S W Q E R T
```

Answer Key

ACTIVITY 4

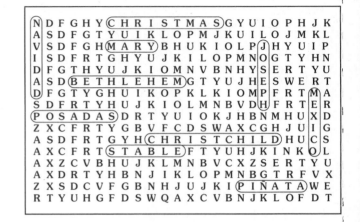

```
N D F G H Y C H R I S T M A S G Y U I O P H J K
A S D F G T Y U I K L O P M J K U I L O J M K L
V S D F G H M A R Y B H U K I O L P J H Y U I P
I S D F R T G H Y U J K I L O P M N O G T Y H N
D F G T H Y U J K I O M N V B N H Y S E R T Y U
A S D B E T H L E H E M G T Y U J H E S W E R T
D F G T Y G H U I K O P K L K I O M P H F R T M A
S D F R T Y H U J K I O L M N B V D H F R T E X
P O S A D A S D R T Y U I O K J H B N M H U J C I
Z X C F R T Y G B V F C D S W A X C G H J U I C G S
A S D F R T G Y H C H R I S T C H I L D H U C S L
A X C F R T S T A B L E F T Y U H J K I N K O L
A X Z C V B H U J K L M N B V C X Z S E R T Y U
A X D R T Y H J N J I K L O P M N B G T R F V X
Z X S D C V F G B N H J U J K I P I Ñ A T A W E
R T Y U H G F D S W Q A X C V B N J K L O F D T
```

ACTIVITY 5

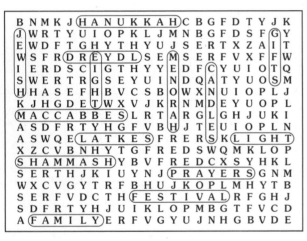

```
B N M K J H A N U K K A H C B G F D T Y J K
J W R T Y U I O P K L J M N B G F D S F G Y
E W D F T G H Y T H Y U J S E R T X Z A I F T
W S F R D R E Y D L S E M S E R F V X F S T Q
I E R D S C I G T H Y Y E D F C Y U I O T S M
S W E R T R G S E Y U I N D Q A T Y U O S L J
H H A S E F H B V C S B O W X N U I O P L J
K J H G D E T W X V J K R N M D E Y U O P L
M A C C A B B E S L R T A R G L G H J U K I
A S D F R T Y H G F V H J T E U I O P L N
A S W Q E L A T K E S F R E R S K L I G H T
X Z C V B N H Y T G F R E D S W Q M K L O P
S H A M M A S H Y B V F R E D C X S Y H K L
S E R T H J K I U Y N J P R A Y E R S G N M
W X C V G Y T R F B H U J K O P L M H Y T B
S E R F V D C T H F E S T I V A L R F G H J
S D F R T Y H J U I K L O P M B G T F V C D
A F A M I L Y E R F V G Y U J N H G B V D E
```

ACTIVITY 6

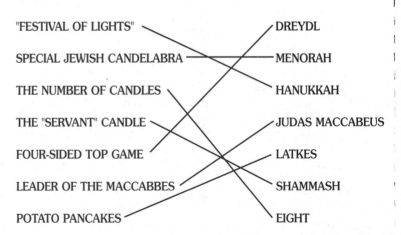

"FESTIVAL OF LIGHTS"	DREYDL
SPECIAL JEWISH CANDELABRA	MENORAH
THE NUMBER OF CANDLES	HANUKKAH
THE "SERVANT" CANDLE	JUDAS MACCABEUS
FOUR-SIDED TOP GAME	LATKES
LEADER OF THE MACCABBES	SHAMMASH
POTATO PANCAKES	EIGHT